THE SENSE OF SELF

THE SENSE OF SELF

A Guide to How We Mature

Lorene A. Stringer

TEMPLE UNIVERSITY PRESS
Philadelphia

Temple University Press, Philadelphia 19122
© 1971 by Temple University. All rights reserved
Published 1971
Printed in the United States of America

International Standard Book Number: 0-87722-008-5
Library of Congress Catalog Card Number: 76-157735

CONTENTS

INTRODUCTION

Twenty years ago mental health professionals who wanted to develop preventive programs had to work hard to find points of entry into the field. Today people in all kinds of work are begging for mental health guidelines. Appeals come from schools and courts and churches, from parent groups and neighborhood centers and welfare agencies. But now that the field of prevention is open to us, we are so filled with doubts and misgivings that we do less advancing than approaching, and less approaching than debating the relative merits of the various approaches that we might make.

Considering how little we know, and how much we do not yet know, we should of course proceed in duly responsible ways. But to be duly responsible means, it seems to me, that we *must* proceed. We must get going, if only to carry our fair share of the burden of our ignorance, because we are not the only people who suffer from our ignorance. Everyone who works responsibly, in whatever capacity, with or for people, is dealing with many unknowns and *is therefore experimenting,* whether by intent or inadvertence, with consistency or inconsistency, and while acknowledging or denying accountability. And because experimenting is always attended with risk of blunders and hurtful effects, this is disquieting knowledge to harbor as one works. It is particularly disquieting and distressing to people who work with children, because children are more plastic and more pervious than adults and are therefore more vulnerable.

The preparation of this material was supported in part by Research Grants MH-188 and MH-14793 from the National Institute of Mental Health, of the National Institutes of Health, United States Public Health Service, and in part by the Mental Health Division of the St. Louis County Health Department.

There is nothing unforgivable about experimenting, however, _provided_ that we evaluate what we do, and learn from our mistakes—in short, that we hold ourselves accountable. But evaluation demands guidelines, one or another kind of conceptual framework within which to develop working hypotheses that can then be tested. We develop these readily enough for our own use, but when it comes to providing them for the use of people without our kinds of training, we have produced remarkably little of value.

Admittedly the task is difficult. The guidelines needed should be (a) simple enough to be readily grasped and easily kept in mind, (b) practical enough, in their implications, to be usable and testable in the field of everyday experience, (c) sophisticated enough to permit discernment of complexities, and (d) encompassing enough to allow for the incorporation of new knowledge, as new knowledge comes. These may well be impossible criteria to satisfy, but they can serve to give direction to our efforts. And we do not have to work alone at the task: we can arrive at sure knowledge sooner, and see theory translated into practice more effectively and adroitly, by offering whatever guidelines we can and enlisting the help of others in testing them in whatever ways they can.

This book began as an attempt to formulate a mental health theory, and to delineate four postulated mental health dimensions (to be discussed in Chapter 1), in such a way as to allow us to carry out a research investigation with some hope that all members of the staff would be operating within similar frames of reference. Before I began to write it, however, I was asked to lead a mental health workshop in the summer of 1963 for elementary teachers and principals, and I used the opportunity to test our emerging research guidelines against the experience of educational practitioners. The material was presented candidly as no more than an effort to develop guidelines, a tentative formulation, to the best of my understanding soundly based on what we know, but embracing much that is not yet proved and may sometime be disproved and meanwhile is wide open to challenge.

The countless and marvelously varying challenges and questions raised by that workshop group and subsequent like groups have done as much to shape the book as have my other resources—the authors whose work I have drawn upon, our hardworking, deeply invested research staff, and all the friends and associates who over the years have so generously shared their thinking with me. A book written in ivory tower seclusion could perhaps be pure of all unconscious plagiarisms and failure to give due credit; this one has grown out of so many interpersonal exchanges that I can no longer account for them all. I can only acknowledge my indebtedness to others in this general way. My indebtedness to the authors who have granted permission for me to refer to their work requires an explicit statement that many of those references are not so much documentation for what I have written as they are invitations to interested readers to explore, in depth and breadth, authoritative sources about fields in which I am no more than a fascinated but often bewildered wanderer.

If the book, as it stands now, appears to be an operational model relating the management of stress to the promotion of psychosocial growth in mental health, it is important to point out that it is still a model of the kind described by D. M. McKay:

> We can think of it as a kind of template which we construct on some hypothetical principles, and then hold up against the real thing in order that the discrepancies between the two may yield fresh information.
>
> This in turn should enable us to modify the template in some respect, after which a fresh comparison may yield further information, and so on. The model, as it were, "subtracts out" at each stage what we think we understand, so that what is not yet understood is revealed more clearly.
>
> You will see at once that we shall judge a good model for this purpose not so much by the success with which it imitates or predicts, but rather by the clarity with which its failures enable us to infer what to modify next (6).

This is the essential process of behavioral science research, but it is also the essential process of good practice in education and in mental health.

THE SENSE OF SELF

Chapter 1. THE CONCEPTUAL FRAMEWORK

To secure us firmly at the outset in the area of our primary concern, which is to learn how to develop and maintain mental health, let me begin by stating the working assumptions on which the conceptual framework of this book is based.

First, mental illness does not typically strike all of a sudden, unpredictably and irremediably. It begins within us, and often its beginnings are imperceptibly small. It increases as a result of neglect or mishandling or misadventure, but its development—far more often than not—is very slow, so that for many months or for many years it may bear little or no resemblance to those blatant disturbances that obviously have to be called *mental illness*. It may never reach that point: mediating circumstances or skilled intervention can completely arrest its development in many cases, and can significantly retard it in many more, allowing us to contain our disturbance and to continue to function in many areas of our lives in more or less normal ways. In short, mental illness becomes doom only when it has become so massive that it overwhelms the whole personality.

Second, and similarly, mental health is neither a God-given birthright nor a stroke of good luck. It, too, begins within us, and increases—given the right conditions. But it, too, develops slowly, requiring many years to become well established. It is always to some degree vulnerable to insult from without. But by the same token it is also open to reinforcement from without. In other words, mental health can be purposefully nurtured.

Third, since these terms, *mental illness* and *mental health,* represent overarching constructs rather than diagnostic entities, it is useful to conceive of them as opposite but constituent parts of the same thing—the psychological state of being. The obvious implication is that in most of us, at

3

any given time, there is some (usually undetermined) degree of mental illness and some degree of mental health. A very large proportion of "mental
illness" would mean psychosis or disabling neurosis; a very small proportion might mean nothing more than a tendency to grow tense and jumpy or
somewhat disorganized under stress. We conceive of the physical state of
being in much the same way: illness can be as great as terminal cancer or
as small as an occasional headache or simple cold. (Neither headaches nor
colds are necessarily of great importance, though the fact remains that a
headache hurts, and a simple cold makes one feel wretched.)

What is not at all obvious is that there is nothing fixed about the proportions of health and illness in any of us, except that they are always
inversely related. For each of us, at any given time, the greater the proportion of mental health, the less the proportion of mental illness; and the
greater the proportion of mental illness, the less the proportion of mental
health. All of us at some time or times suffer some degree of mental illness,
and most of us at some times enjoy some degree of mental health.

There is an important implication in this inverse relationship, particularly when it is taken in conjunction with another point—namely, that
while these proportions vary over time, they vary less as we grow older, as
accumulating life experience lends its weight more to the one or the other
and slows down the tendency to change. In terms of our working assumptions, we have until very recently concentrated our efforts upon trying to
decrease mental illness by treating mental illness. We have not to any significant degree tried the other obvious possibility, of attempting to decrease
mental illness by increasing mental health. We have chosen to work against
accumulated life experience of sufficient weight to be almost immovable;
and we have put almost no effort at all into trying to shape the accumulating life experience while it is still open to change, as it is in the very young.
The tremendously hard work that has gone on in hospitals, clinics, and
laboratories has brought substantial gains in knowledge and in resources
for treatment, but in spite of these gains mental illness has continued to
increase far faster than our ability to deal with it. It seems to me that it has
become imperative that we address ourselves to the study of mental *health*
and the ways in which it can be reinforced.

At this point some pertinent distinctions should be made. Although I
used the idea of the inverse proportions of mental health and mental illness
first in reference to an individual, and for the most part shall be talking
about individuals from here on, the same concept is applicable to social
systems—to school districts, to schools, to classrooms, to families. In each of
these social systems, as in each of us individually, there is at every point in
time some undetermined proportion of mental health and some proportion

of mental illness, some people who appear to be quite healthy, and some who seem quite disturbed. Common sense, of course, tells us that we cannot effectively use the same approach to these two different groups in social systems; nor can we use the same approach to the two different kinds of people. The appropriate model for working with mental illness is the psychiatric model; the appropriate one for working with mental health is what we are nowadays calling the "social competence model." The psychiatric model develops in the field of psychiatry; the social competence model develops first in the family, but continues in the field of education.

There are intrinsic and essential differences in the kinds of work that go on in these two fields, in focus, in method, and in aim. In the psychiatric field the focus is primarily and sometimes exclusively on the patient's feelings; the method is usually that of some form of psychotherapy, perhaps most often the one-to-one relationship of therapist and patient; and the aim is to help the patient to resolve his emotional conflicts well enough to enable him to function somewhat more happily and productively than before. In the field of education the primary focus is on the student's intellect; the method is that of cognitive learning, using the (roughly) thirty-to-one ratio between students and teacher; and the appropriate (if still largely unrecognized) aim in relation to mental health is the primary prevention of mental illness—dealing so effectively with trivial problems that they don't become major problems—which necessarily involves the positive nurturing of mental health.

The two fields seem to be clearly distinct, with nothing to indicate any traffic between them. There is traffic between them, however—child traffic. Many kinds of emotional problems interfere with cognitive learning, making it impossible for the children so afflicted to benefit from what the school has to offer, to be immunized against mental illness, as it were, through the process of education (it is my belief, and Glidewell's, that a good education in the fullest sense does constitute a sort of immunization against mental illness), so that the children can grow more steadily toward mental health. These are the children who need to cross over to the field of psychiatry, to the child guidance clinic or the private psychiatrist, the residential treatment center or the hospital, there to receive—if they are lucky—the kind of treatment that will make it possible for them to resume (or, for some, to begin) the cognitive learning that alone can enable them to become socially competent adults.

For many years this kind of child traffic has been as heavy as our psychiatric facilities could handle, and still the amount of unmet need is appalling. Glidewell and Swallow (3), in their 1968 Report to the Joint Commission on the Mental Health of Children, made a conservative estimate based on the 1960 census figures, that there were 3 million children between five and twelve years of age who needed some professional (psychiatric) help, and 1.3 million who would have been referred to psychiatric facilities if such facilities had been available. It is unrealistic to hope that we can expand our psychiatric facilities enough to deal effectively with a problem of this size. We must therefore intensify our efforts to develop the potential of our schools for the early detection and the primary prevention of mental illness in children. We shall have a lot of sick children, even so: we have found in our St. Louis County studies that the sickest children in our schools were already sick before they entered school (10). Moreover, we seem now to be adding to the evidence that even with mental health intervention in the earliest school years (Kindergarten through Grade II) it is very difficult to achieve significant improvement in children's mental health on a case-by-case basis, and it seems to grow more difficult after the Kindergarten year. The educational process, if our small study is generalizable to so broad a term, appears to strengthen the health of children who enter with adequate coping strengths, but it appears to offer little or nothing that helps to develop the health of weaker, more vulnerable children. We must find some way to strengthen the children who are at risk, and the necessary first step toward doing that is to learn more about how children grow and what forces affect them in what ways.

Now we have postulated that mental illness increases and that this increase can be arrested or retarded, and that mental health also increases and that this increase can be assisted; and then I said that there was nothing fixed or unvarying about the proportions of health and illness that each of us might contain, except that they were always inversely related, and that their tendency to vary in time was slowed down by the accumulating life experience. We have a semantic difficulty to deal with here. The question is whether we are talking about something that changes as the human infant does, going through successive stages of growth and finally reaching maturity, or about something that changes as bank accounts do, increasing at some times, decreasing at others. The easiest way to achieve clarification, and perhaps at the same time to move toward a working definition of mental health, is to consider in some detail the growth process involved in an infant's progressive physical development toward and into adulthood. Note, to begin with, that a newborn infant responds globally to whatever stimulates him to a response (4). Whether he is hungry or startled or hurting or hot or cold or merely restless, he cries—and he cries with all of him, legs and arms waving, skin flushing, muscles tensing, lungs working like bellows. Adults normally respond quite differently to such stimuli. They perceive the stimuli as different and react selectively to deal with them as best they can under the circumstances involved. Secondly, physical growth can be described as change in the direction of increasing differentiation of perception and of reaction, gradually providing more freedom of action, a wider range of choice among alternatives, greater flexibility and adaptation, and thus, presumably, more control over what we do. (Incidentally, when these same attributes are translated into psychological terms, they are those that best distinguish the mentally healthy from the mentally ill.)

To discern how this change toward greater differentiation comes about, it is helpful to borrow concepts and paraphrase part of the content of Hans Selye's book entitled *The Stress of Life* (7). Each of us begins life with (a) a given biological potential, (b) a strong drive toward homeostasis, and (c) an environment. The biological potential is the capacity to develop from the impregnated ovum to the fully mature human being. It is a reservoir of energy to change, to enlarge, and to become increasingly complex and differentiated in structure and in functioning. Obviously a tremendous amount of energy is locked up in the biological potential: but it is not an unlimited amount of energy. At the beginning, in the instant of conception, it is limited only by hereditarily determined boundaries; but with the very first cell division an interaction process begins, so that in effect each of the divided-cell parts becomes an "environment" for the other. As cell division continues, what the Eidusons and their colleagues call the "intraorganismic environment" becomes increasingly complex (1). Very quickly the prenatal environment begins to determine more specifically the ways in which the genetically given potential may develop, and the ways in which it may not. Later, the postnatal environment adds further specific determinants, including (necessarily) limitations. But there is a peculiarity about those limitations that is worth noting: we never know—in the course of a lifetime—just where they are. Not until death supervenes can we say with certainty that the limits have been reached.

(There is one astonishing, miraculous exception to the gradual exhaustion of the energy reservoir by the process of living. For each individual the ultimate exhaustion is inevitable, but the process of living may include the process of reproducing, and procreation is literally the creation of an entirely new and different biological potential with its own reservoir of energy.)

Joined with the biological potential is the homeostatic drive, operating in a multitude of ways to make or keep us comfortable. Its aim is to safeguard our well-being by keeping in play an extraordinary system of checks and balances, both to resist any kind of change that would lessen our comfort, and to seek any kind of change that would lessen discomfort. There is, for example, the homeostatic mechanism that defends us against environmental heat or cold by maintaining the constancy of our body temperature. The same mechanism defends us against infection by stimulating hormonal production to combat the infection. Another such mechanism regulates the composition of our blood, accommodating it to normal variations in our diet, but changing it defensively in the presence of active disease. All such operations require an expenditure of energy, whether to resist change or to produce it; but most of the time we are quite unconscious of expending energy in this way—we merely recognize the point at which we again attain comfort and equilibrium, and mark it by drawing a deep breath and relaxing.

At best, however, our equilibrium is never more than quasi-stable. Stressors impinge upon it from both inside and outside, some of them mildly, some severely, but few predictably. From inside, the biological potential, always seeking to actualize itself, pushes us to develop, to change, to become different from what we are now. From outside, from our environment, other people push us to change, demanding more of us than we want to give, or refusing to give us as much as we want from them. Let any stressor become severe enough, and it will do two things: first, it will upset our quasi-stable equilibrium, and second, in Selye's words, it will trigger "a purposeful, homeostatic reaction" in us, a stress response that is a *somehow* attempt to get out from under, to recover our balance, and to find comfort again. This is the basic pattern of adaptation, essentially the same whether it describes the imperceptible, unconscious adjustments that we make a thousand times a day, or the comeback—after a massive assault—that it may take us years to accomplish.

In case it escaped attention, I may as well acknowledge frankly that while I am talking here of the biological potential as actualizing itself in both the physical and the psychological modalities, I can cite no specific work that fully and explicitly supports my doing this. Such investigations as I know of (2, 5, 7, 12) have turned up exciting leads in this direction, offering promise that sometime, and perhaps fairly soon, we may understand exactly how the interchange of energy takes place between physiological and psychological processes; but for the present we are still short of full and exact understanding. Meanwhile, I am simply going on the evidence of common experience: since severely stressful emotions, such as grief or rage or fear or jealousy or simple suspense, can leave us feeling exhausted even though to all appearance we have been quiescent, it seems reasonable to think that the biological potential is the source of energy for whatever kind of work we do, whether physical, intellectual, or emotional, voluntary or involuntary.

At this point it may seem that we are left at the mercy of whatever stressors confront us, because dealing with stress of any kind requires work and uses energy, and we have only a limited though indeterminate amount of energy at our disposal. We are inclined to interpret the word *stress* in an almost exclusively negative way. But there is nothing against our using it with broader meaning, to denote anything—any pressure or excitement— that impels us to move from one position to another. Understood thus, stress can include such things as stimulation, interest, ambition, eagerness, curiosity—in short, many of the aspects of growing that are pleasurable. I am not sure that in the absence of all stress we should just stagnate happily in equilibrium (I rather suspect that unless from day to day we "ripe and ripe," we might find that from day to day we rot and rot), but it is quite clear that when we are speaking of *stress* in the broader sense, <u>stress is essential to growth</u>.

We should note here, at least in passing, that there are two different basic orientations to stress, one the passive-adaptive, and the other the active-coping. Neither orientation is "pure" and inviolable, but making the distinction seems necessary because throughout these discussions we shall be focusing on the active-coping orientation to the almost total neglect of the passive-adaptive. This is not just a cavalier writing-off of passive-adaptive people as not worth noticing; it is a matter of my not yet understanding them well enough to discern how they fit (if they fit) into this conceptual framework. My tentative impression is that a passive adaptation is always at least a temporary, and sometimes a permanent, capitulation at the expense of the growth impulse, and results in delayed or arrested development of some aspect of the personality; but the question needs more careful investigation.

In returning to the idea of stress as essential to growth, we should note that stress is not, of course, all that is essential. Growth, defined as change toward increasing differentiation of structure and of functioning, involves change over time in the efficiency of our responses to stress. It is not, as we might like to imagine it, a simple, straightforward, effortless outflowing of the biological potential. Rather, it is progression by way of repeated alternations of rest and thrust, of balance and imbalance, of security and risk, like walking, which someone has defined as a progressive series of aborted falls. Between steps we are precariously balanced, no matter on which foot we are poised; but by accepting the risk, and exerting the necessary energy, we can move ourselves from one place to another. I am always tempted to suggest, further, that we can get there faster, wherever "there" is, by running than by walking, but at increased risk of taking a fall; and (in line with the "ripe or rot" idea) we can of course lessen the risk by standing still instead of walking, and lessen it still further by sitting or lying down, but none of these alternatives takes us anywhere. The analogy poses a difficulty in seeming to imply that we can grow or not grow as we choose, or can grow slowly or rapidly at will. We shall deal with that difficulty later, but if we set it aside for the moment, perhaps we can find the analogy useful in understanding the growth process.

Until we have learned rather more than we know now, we almost have to consider one kind of human growth at a time, as if one kind were really separable from another. There has been developed in this way a considerable body of knowledge about physical growth. A study reported by Shuttleworth documents the alternations of acceleration and deceleration in physical growth, occurring in two major cycles: first, tremendously rapid growth from conception to birth, followed by marked deceleration over the next eight to twelve or fourteen years (weight is multiplied by over 157,000 times in the eight months preceding birth, by only three times in the twelve months following birth, and by decreasing factors in the following years); and second, a slight acceleration of growth with the onset of adolescence, followed by another marked slowing down as the adolescent nears adult size. The general course is as simple as running, slowing to a walk (perhaps even to a brief standstill), and then quickening pace again, and again slowing down. It poses no problem until we try to account for it. Consider this paragraph from the Shuttleworth report:

> In brief, our theory is that the patterns of physical growth shown by the [twenty-two] different dimensions and different groups from conception to maturity are the resultant of a progressive balancing of endocrine factors, of factors peculiar to each dimension, of factors determining mature size, and of factors associated with sex. Each of these factors represents an exceedingly complex set of forces, some of which operate persistently throughout the growth span, while others operate for only limited intervals and at different ages. None act independently. All are inexorably entangled by their mutual action and interaction in a single continuous process. An observed growth pattern is the external manifestation of the constantly shifting balance of such underlying forces (8).

It seems reasonable to expect that other kinds of growth, when they have been as thoroughly investigated, will prove to be similarly complex, involving a number of factors, each representing an "exceedingly complex set of forces" operating differentially but always interdependently. Psychosocial "growth," which somehow has to encompass physical growth, will be still more complex. But even in such elaborations we shall be dealing essentially, I think, with the same familiar elements: where Shuttleworth speaks of forces and constant shifting and a progressive balancing, we speak of stresses and stress responses and the homeostatic drive.

There are, however, three respects in which psychosocial growth is strikingly different from physical growth. First, we can be quite confident that a child who is four feet tall today will not become three feet ten inches tall tomorrow or next month or next year. This irreversibility is not true of psychosocial growth. A child who today is generous and thoughtful toward others may become, a month hence, greedy and inconsiderate. A child who today is adequately responsible may be quite irresponsible again tomorrow. The patterns of psychosocial growth include not only alternations of acceleration and deceleration, but also alternations of progression and regression—a procedure that is like taking two steps forward, one step back, and two steps forward again. Such regression, which would be appallingly pathological in physical growth, occurs so frequently in psychosocial growth that it must be considered part of the normal pattern, functionally a homeostatic mechanism (9).

But—and this the second difference—compared to the homeostatic mechanisms of the body, psychological regression looks like a grossly wasteful, risky, *somehow* attempt to get out from under stress by pulling back to a position of earlier comfort. If there is to be renewed advance, the ground thus lost will have to be regained, which would seem to suggest that twice as much effort and energy will be required; and the only alternative to redoubled effort is more regression—toward or into pathology. Beneath this evident disadvantage, however, there is a potential advantage. The homeostats that regulate body temperature and blood composition require no conscious effort at all. There is nothing of the *somehow* in them; they are superb automata operating with precision and economy. But by the same token they are pretty well out of the reach of conscious control. We may believe that a little fever is helpful in combating infections, but few of us can just think ourselves into a little fever. We might prefer to look cool and immaculate on a hot day, but few of us can stop sweating by merely trying not to sweat. Yet if we know that getting today's work done today will make tomorrow's work easier, we can by conscious effort get ourselves up and moving in the mornings, even though we might very much like to stay in bed. If we believe that our friends deserve courtesy from us, we can by conscious effort deal courteously with them, even when—inside—we are feeling angry with the whole world. Thus in psychosocial growth there is an element of voluntary control not present in physical growth—at least, there is something that looks like room for the exercise of choice, to grow or

not to grow, to cope actively with stress in order to move ahead, or to surrender passively to it and regress.

And this foreshadows the third difference—that physical growth is
usually completed within the first two decades of life, but that psychosocial
growth can continue throughout the whole life span, if an individual so
chooses.

The question now becomes: What determines that choice? Why do we
at some times cope effectively with stress, and grow as a result, and at other
times lapse into regression? When we know (as most of us do know, if we
stop to think) that to regress is likely to mean double trouble, why should
we ever regress? The answer that suggests itself sounds simple: Since coping with stress requires energy, what we "choose" to do must be determined by (a) the amount of energy needed for dealing with the specific
stressor, and (b) the amount of energy available to us at that particular
time. If we have energy adequate to the need, our stress response will be
active coping, directed toward establishing a new equilibrium at a higher,
freer level. If our energy is inadequate to the need, our stress response will
be some kind of regressive (or passive) adaptation. There are only three
main forms of these regressive adaptations (to be considered below), but
there is an important point to be made first about the energy-ratio issue.

The implications of this issue are quite different for children and for
adults. Children have their physical growth to contend with, and they have
no control over it; they cannot turn it off or on at need, and therefore its
demands for energy take priority over any other demands. Unless we recognize this and make adequate allowance for it in the context of the other
demands we make upon children, we run a serious risk of forcing them into
deficit functioning.

With adults, who no longer have to reckon with the energy demands of
physical growth, the implications are primarily psychosocial. If we have
energy enough to exercise voluntary control over what we do at the points
of choice (which are most frequently the points of stress), then we can use
stress to achieve progress toward greater differentiation of perception and
reaction, toward more degrees of freedom, more alternatives to choose
among, more personal resources—in short, toward increasing mental
health. If we do not have energy enough to exercise voluntary control at the
points of choice, then stress uses us, forcing us to seek equilibrium again at
some level of lesser differentiation, decreased freedom, fewer alternatives,
and diminished personal resources—in short, decreasing the proportion of
mental health and increasing the proportion of mental illness within us.

The most natural form of such noncoping is frank regression—really
moving back, as it were, along the line of our growth, to some position

formerly comfortable and currently still tenable, although perhaps at the expense of feeling some shame and guilt, and perhaps incurring the censure of others, because—take us by and large—we do not look kindly upon frankly regressive behavior. You have seen this in the eight-year-old who under a given kind of stress behaves like a three-year-old, or in the adult who suddenly erupts into a display of childish petulance or crude self-seeking.

If one feels—for whatever reason—*forbidden* to regress, but at the same time does not have energy adequate for successful coping, the stalemate can be resolved by shunting the stress from the psychological arena into either the somatic or the social arena.

Given energy enough, the alternatives are: to bull one's way through the stressor, to explore it long and hard enough to find a way to get over it or under it or around it (in any case effectively coping with it), or to retreat from it by one of three possible regressive ways—frank regression, psychosomatic illness, or unloading the stress onto someone else.

It has to be said that psychosomatic illness as a stress response offers certain unique advantages. It is still, at present, socially acceptable where more frankly regressive behavior is not. It can excuse us from performing, it may even by prescription relieve us of responsibility (a doctor may tell us firmly and authoritatively to stay in bed for at least a week), and it allows for our enjoying that relief with less guilt because we pay for it with pain or restriction of freedom. Its disadvantage is that, once the voluntary control has been abdicated, and the stressor has found a compliant body organ or organ system to work upon, it is extremely difficult to reverse the process and regain voluntary control. It may be unnecessary to add that proneness to accidents and perhaps low resistance to infections belong in this same category (4).

When the stress is shunted into the social arena, the result is the most peculiar and most nearly untreatable form of mental illness, because the person who initially feels the stress proceeds to unload it onto someone else, thereby gaining relief enough to feel no need of treatment. In its milder forms we call this "scapegoating"; in its most dangerous forms we call it paranoia: but whatever the degree of severity, the basic operation is the same. By finding and targeting an innocent victim, the sick person becomes in his own eyes no longer sick, but strong and able and absolutely *right*. Some parents scapegoat their children in this way, some employers scapegoat an employee, and here and there in a classroom we find a bright child who repeatedly gets his classmates in trouble without himself ever breaking a classroom rule.

Both the scapegoating and the psychosmatic disorders involve what my friend Fran Porter used to call *slitching,* a combination of *slip* and *switch*, with a distinct overtone of unintentionally-on-purpose. Both may well be more costly in the long run than the frank psychological regression that they substitute for. We may some day consider, as Dr. Quentin Rae-Grant has suggested, that one good measure of mental health is the reversible fluidity of frank regression, the ease and comfort with which one can regress instead of slitching, and then recover and progress again. Certainly not all frank regression is to be condemned or contemned. To go to sleep when we are really too tired to cope further on some particular day, to take a vacation when we need one, to use coffee breaks to interrupt the tensions that build up during the work day—all of these are perfectly healthy regressions, *provided only* that they are followed by a return to coping when they have restored our energy to coping level.

Whatever the outcome of our engagements with stress, the crucial determinant of the outcome is energy—specifically, the ratio of available energy to needed energy. Sometimes we can estimate the need in advance and to a degree prepare for it, as when we go to school for the first time, or start in a new job, or get married. Unfortunately, though, we are often unable to predict how much energy may be needed at any given time. In part, this is because many of the stressors that impinge upon us are not foreseeable: accidents and financial reverses and sudden bereavements do occur, and sometimes a beautiful and longed-for opportunity opens up all unexpectedly. To complicate matters further, many stressors are invisible as well as unforeseeable, being combinations or accumulations of forces, each in itself too mild to be recognized as pressure, but collectively strong enough to precipitate a stress response. For example, a small child's bid for a little adult attention is no great demand; but spend your day, as teachers do, with thirty small children, giving just a little to each of them, and then drive home and—as in the old, tired TV commercial— find a tricycle in your driveway, and you produce a stress response: but the stressor is not merely the tricycle in the driveway—it is the tricycle on top of the sum of the entire day's demands.

Notice that in this same situation we are involved not only with visible and invisible stressors, but also with internal and external stressors. In the course of such a day of giving to a whole roomful of children, we are almost sure to reach a point at which we don't *want* to give any more; and from that point on we have to struggle with an internal stressor, a perfectly natural but professionally unacceptable impulse to say, "The heck with all of you youngsters! I'm tired of you, I've had it with you— now leave me alone!" And we struggle more or less successfully to curb that impulse, but then we find the external stressor (the trike in the driveway), and we blow. Every one who makes any claim to being "civilized" copes daily with such internal stressors, our own impulses, our own needs, trying in fact to *keep* them invisible to others; and this has social consequences, too, which deserve consideration.

In one notable respect the invisible stressors are more pernicious than those that are unforeseeable but become perfectly visible when they occur. We understand and allow for the regression when we recognize the precipitating stressor. We offer sympathy and support to the child who has lost a parent, broken a leg, or even merely lost or broken a toy. We are all too likely to feel just exasperated with a child who on a given day can seem to do nothing right and who grows steadily angrier and nearer to tears with every passing hour. When we can't see the stressor, we tend to see the stress response as willful misbehavior intended to annoy or defy, and calling rather for forceful restriction than for sympathy and support. The visible stressors, like physical illness, bring our friends to our aid and thereby often make it easier for us to recover. The invisible stressors, like mental illnesses, alienate, and leave us unbefriended, unhelped, and only the worse off for being thus rejected.

There is likewise a difference between our reactions to sudden stress and our reactions to chronic stress, even when both are perfectly visible. It is one thing—and important in its own right—to respond helpfully and courageously to a sudden emergency. It is quite another thing to stay with a demanding and distressing situation, helpfully and courageously, day after day, week after week, sometimes year after year. Our friends note with admiration any demonstrated capacity to cope adequately with emergency situations, and their admiration is strongly supportive to us. But the capacity to handle the long-drawn-out, chronic stress situation is likely to go unnoticed and unsupported, except by the unusually perceptive, understanding few. The duration of the stress is doubtless one of the factors accounting for our generally quicker recovery from emergencies than from the chronic demands, but it is not, I think, the only factor: the regard of our friends is a stimulant to recovery, while their disregard impedes it.

Yet we can learn in time, one would hope, to react more rationally and constructively both to stressors and to our own stress responses, whether or not the stressors are visible, whether or not they are chronic, and whether or not our stress responses tend to be coping, regressive, or slitching. Nevertheless, these are all after-the-fact transactions. We shall still not be able to predict with any accuracy how much energy will be needed at any given time.

Thus, if we are concerned about psychosocial growth and mental health, it is clearly imperative that we try to ensure that we have an adequate amount of energy available for the unforeseeable needs. This means that we must somehow learn to build up a reserve, to develop and maintain a surplus over and above the amount required for everyday living and growing, to keep a safe balance in the bank, as it were. Let me restate this in a slightly different way, in order to tie together the beginning and the end of my argument: We can learn how to increase and safeguard mental health if we can learn to use enough energy to transmute stress into growth, while conserving or regaining enough energy to build a reserve against unforeseeable demands.

It is possible, we think, to build such a reserve by developing certain psychosocial resources that in one way or another will improve the efficiency of our stress responses. In our St. Louis County Studies (11) we have been working with four such (postulated) resources, and I shall be discussing each of them in turn from here on. We are by no means prepared to maintain that, taken together, these four resources constitute all the necessary and sufficient conditions of mental health, but there is a rationale for each, running approximately as follows.

First, moving under stress from one position to another always involves some risk; awareness of risk arouses anxiety; and anxiety is energy-consuming. Anything, therefore, that supports and sustains us during stress, steadying us from the time we leave one comfortable, entrenched position until we manage to secure another position, will increase the amount of energy available for growth. We propose that the psychosocial resource best suited to do this, all the way from birth to death, is what we commonly call *good interpersonal relationships,* the close and strong ties with people who can be counted upon for support and encouragement in the times of our need.

Second, whenever the use of our energy is involuntarily determined, as when one's invariable reaction to stress is to cope or to regress or to somatize or to scapegoat someone else, much of the energy spent will be wasted, bringing us little or no returns in growth or in any other gains of consequence. Anything, therefore, that enables us to exercise voluntary control at the points of choice, both to engage with stress whenever we stand to gain by coping and to disengage ourselves from stress whenever the game isn't worth the candle, will increase the amount of energy available to us for growth or for reserve. We propose that the psychosocial resource that can most effectively aid us here is a *healthy self-esteem,* a quiet but sturdy confidence in our ability to chart our own course and to correct our mistakes as we go along.

Third, while effective coping with stress always uses energy, the amount required can be reduced in direct proportion to the number and degree of relevant skills that can be applied to the coping effort. Anything, therefore, that enables us to substitute skills for sweat in our coping efforts will leave more energy available for investment in further ventures. We propose that the psychosocial resource most apt to achieve this economy is what we call in our office jargon C-P-R, meaning *competence, productivity,* and *responsibility,* the skills and the practiced and disciplined use of skills that can change to advantage things in the world around us.

Fourth, since the energy required for effective coping is related also to the severity of the stress, it is eminently worthwhile to explore for ways of perforating and puncturing stress, to diminish its severity. Anything, therefore, that can bring us momentary relief or elation may be in fact the most versatile, potent, and restorative of all stress responses—and the least expensive. We propose that the only psychosocial resource that can serve us in this way is a *large capacity for enjoyment.*

Propositions, of course, are worth making only if they provoke challenge, induce thoughtful and intensive analysis, and lead in time to the formulation of hypotheses testable both in the research laboratory and in the field of practice. Whether these propositions can do so much remains to be seen. If they cannot, they are replaceable by any more salient constructs that can be developed. Meanwhile, they at least stake out for us a significant area for investigation of the multiple intricate interweavings of stress and growth.

Chapter **2. THE SUSTAINING NETWORK**

Before a more detailed consideration of our postulated psychosocial resources, an important point should be made explicit that has been left implicit until now. It has to do with the uses of information.

If a resource is of value and therefore worth our seeking to acquire, it is also an idea in our heads that we want to see actualized in the world outside of us. The question is how to go about actualizing it. Gregory Bateson (1) has put the issue delightfully in a passage that I am going to paraphrase. If, he says, what is in your head is an idea of the breakfast you want—for example, bacon and eggs arranged side by side upon a plate—you can't expect to get it just by waiting for the random or natural course of events to unfold. On the contrary, you have to expect a number of interferences in the natural or random course of events: someone has to interfere with the natural juxtaposition of hen and egg, and of pig and feeding trough; someone has to transform pig into bacon and box the eggs; perhaps someone else transports them to market, where another someone else buys them and takes them to restaurant or home, where perhaps still another person fries them, puts them on a plate, and takes them to table. Only after all of these interferences have taken place is congruence achieved between what was in your head and what is now in the world outside of you.

Thus, in value-seeking, Bateson says, we try to alter what is in the world outside in such a way as to make it conform to something in our heads. In information-seeking we do just the reverse: we achieve congruence between what is in our heads and what is in the world outside of us by studying that world, by trying to perceive patterns in it, and perceiving them there, by altering the patterns in our heads accordingly.

Both processes are salient in our concerns here. Most of the time we get

18

what we want by working for it, by interfering in the natural course of events in such a way as to achieve "an otherwise improbable outcome" (1); and our chances of achieving such an outcome are greatly improved when our interferences are based on valid information about what is in the world outside of us. There are, of course, occasions of "serendipity," when we gain something of value in the course of searching for something else; but these are rare. We cannot reasonably look either to serendipity or the natural course of events to bestow upon us the resources that we want or need. We can reasonably look to our own efforts, if they are intelligently directed.

There is a further implication worth noting. When we come out the losers in our psychosocial ventures, we commonly tend to blame the outcome on our having done something wrong somewhere along the line; but the sorry outcomes could just as well be due to our having done nothing when we should have been taking some positive action, based on sound information, to help us to achieve the desired outcome. Clearly, our first concern must be to gain sound information—specifically, here, about interpersonal relationships.

Because this subject is enormously complex, I am going to focus primarily on only one aspect of it. When we speak of interpersonal relationships as a sustaining network capable of supporting us during stress, we are obviously speaking of dependency relationships, and at least by implication we are acknowledging dependency needs. These are remarkably unpopular subjects in our society, and to judge even from our professional literature one would assume that all dependency needs are pathological if they persist beyond the age of three to five years, that they should be shed along the way precisely as we shed our baby teeth, and preferably at about the same age. The error involved in that attitude is a simple one, which probably accounts for its being so generally overlooked: it is *unmet* dependency needs that are pathological, that tend to leak into and poison all kinds of relationships, at all chronological ages from birth to death. There is no evidence to suggest that dependency needs *per se* are pathological.

But if, to avoid becoming pathologically dependent, we have to make sure that all of our dependency needs are met, we have a problem. Having all of our dependency needs met presupposes the constant availability of someone willing and able to meet them, someone who is dependable. But who of us is either willing or able to be always dependable and never dependent? For that matter, what healthy person is willing to be always dependent and never depended upon? Our dependency needs change from time to time, and our capacity to be dependable also changes. Our sustaining network, therefore, must be defined as a set of interdependencies that allow us to be dependent when we need to be, but oblige us at other times to be dependable.

If this suggests to you, as it does to me, that all of our significant inter-personal relationships are—like marriage—in the nature of contracts, then we have to add that most of them are very odd contracts, indeed, signalized by no ceremony, with no terms specified, and often with each of the parties involved having his own private version of what are his rights and what are the other person's obligations. Such unacknowledged contracts are well suited to produce disappointment, resentment, bitterness, and guilt, under-mining if not effectively destroying relationships. This is certainly not to say that a ceremony or a public exchange of promises, or duly witnessed and notarized signatures to a written agreement, can guarantee the quality and duration of a relationship. It is only to say that the real source of trou-ble is those private versions of contract terms that we usually prefer not to communicate and often not even to recognize. An obvious inference is that we keep those private versions hidden, even from ourselves, out of shame or some other defense mechanism, because we tend to hope for more from the other person than we are prepared to give in exchange.

An equally obvious implication is that open communication might go far toward helping us to develop our interpersonal relationships to their fullest potential. I am using the term *open communication* loosely here and very broadly; I would include under this definition anything and everything that contributes to our clearer and more exact understanding of ourselves and others, and to our ability to exchange that understanding with others. We have many different words to denote all the kinds of things thus includ-ed, but they can be covered succinctly: there are just four kinds of essential communication skills: verbal-expressive, verbal-receptive, nonverbal-expressive, and nonverbal-receptive. The verbal-expressive skills enable us to formulate ideas, give names to feelings, shape experiences into learnings, and by these means begin to understand ourselves and convey our ideas and feelings effectively to others. The verbal-receptive skills (of good listening) enable us to share the ideas and feelings of others, to learn from their experiences as well as from our own, and by these means begin to under-stand others. The nonverbal-expressive skills help us to convey the mean-ings that we can't quite fit into words, meanings that would be distorted or diminished if they were encased in words. Let me add, to make a point, that there is often a willy-nilly component in some of our nonverbal-expressive communications: our behavior, our posture, our gait, gestures, tone of voice, manner of dress—all of these things often speak for us when we might wish they wouldn't. The point is that by no means all of our communications reflect communication *skills*. Many are as involuntary as a tic or a sneeze. Finally, the nonverbal-receptive skills help us to glimpse what is meant, whether it goes along with or counter to the words that are said.

We tend to pay little attention to three out of these four kinds of communication skills. We emphasize the verbal-expressive skills, but devote little effort to developing listening skills, and practically no effort at all to maintaining and better understanding the nonverbal skills. And yet those usually overlooked, disparaged, and mistrusted nonverbal communications are the ones that can make or break interpersonal relationships, depending upon whether the messages get through or not. Since most of us are pretty well indoctrinated with the idea that emotional dependency is something to be ashamed of, we talk little or not at all about our dependency needs; but this neither eliminates nor weakens them. Unless we have the nonverbal skills to aid us in such relationships by keeping us attuned to the wordless feelings that count for so much, misunderstanding is piled on misunderstanding, unrecognized lie is added to unrecognized lie, until all communication ends, and the relationship breaks.

One major part of our task here, then, will be to try to find our way through such common misunderstandings and unrecognized lies to the feelings that they so effectively obscure. The other major part will be to try to trace (as it were) the natural history of human dependency needs, by following one hypothetical person through the series of transitions that are involved in even an *optimal* course from infancy to old age. Like dependency needs, old age is not a popular subject; but if we live long enough, we grow old, and if we grow old, better to grow old gracefully, and if by growing old gracefully, we mean (as I suspect we do) that we learn to make minimal demands of other people, while accepting gratefully whatever others give, and somehow maintaining a cheerful demeanor throughout, then we shall do well to look at the full size of the tasks involved. How and when and by what combinations of stressors and coping strengths does the total dependency of the earliest years become the increasing self-dependence of early adulthood that later may grow into dependability in our mature years? And when in later years our reserves of strength and energy are depleted, and our recuperative powers have largely gone, how do we manage to retire from the field of being dependable and depended upon, and learn to deal with our own dependency needs? Even a bare outline makes it crystal clear that the essential tasks of growth in interpersonal relationships span the whole lifetime.

For a simple beginning, let us make our hypothetical protagonist a first child, and—to illuminate a couple of cultural issues—a male. In our society both the earliest years of child-rearing and most of the early years of schooling are left predominantly in the hands of women; and particularly in relation to male dependency needs I think we tend—with an able assist from most men—to make two errors: first, to ask too much too soon, giving many little boys a rough time trying to live up to what is demanded of them, and then to compound that difficulty by asking too little too late, inviting all too many young men to stop short of ever becoming dependable. We do better in this respect by girls; we permit (and a good many men like to encourage) a considerable dependency in females. But while males are fully as vulnerable as females to the stresses that at times precipitate either regression or dependence on someone else for a helping hand, we proscribe such dependency in males, at least from the age of two or three years. The consequences of this particular double standard are, I think, costlier to all of us, male and female alike, than we realize. At any rate, if we are going to say (as some people do) that after age forty women are practically indestructible, it seems pertinent to ask if this may be in some part due to their greater ease and comfort in acknowledging and dealing with their dependency needs.

Beyond this point I shall not be making any great issue of sex differences; they will be mentioned whenever they are involved in a point worth making, but in the matter of interpersonal relationships and dependency needs, there are more likenesses than differences between the two sexes. And whenever in what follows, I say "parents," you are free to take it as meaning parents or father or mother or any other person in the parental role.

The Early Relationships

A good marriage begins with two happy, healthy young people who in certain essential respects complement each other, and who in certain other ways parallel each other. Within a year or two they achieve a reasonably stable and mutually satisfying conjugal relationship; in short, they reach a comfortable homeostatic equilibrium in their marriage. They look forward with deep interest to having children, they plan when to have their first child, and—give or take a few months—matters go according to plan. But the fact of discovering that they are now expectant parents is a stressor that upsets the homeostatic balance of their marriage. They have to make room in their relationship for a third individual, a new and unknown third; and in the process of making room they experience, each of them separately, and both of them together, the shifting balance of underlying forces in them. The biological potential of their marriage, by beginning to actualize itself, compels them to change: they not only start growing into parenthood, but also start learning how to continue their partnership under the now-changed terms of their contract.

They have coping strengths enough, however, to transmute this stress into growth, so that they become welcoming parents. When the child is born, he is for a few days a source of pure joy and pride to them, a fine surplus in their psychological economy. And this is fortunate, because they are going to need a surplus. They are about to be subjected to a new stress —more accurately, a triple stress.

First, this infant, who for nine months has been carried along on a completely automated program of development that continuously supplied his needs (not without cost to his mother, but not requiring thought on her part, nor even in fact her consent), is now suddenly and totally dependent upon his parents to supply his needs, which means first that his parents must perceive these needs accurately, and then that they be both willing and able to meet them. This is a much more troubling dependency than that of the not-yet-born, about whom the parents never had to ask themselves, Is he warm enough? Is he cool enough? Is he wet? Is he dry? Did he nurse enough? Is he asleep yet? Is he safe, there in the other room? and How soon will he need to be fed again?

Moreover, the newborn's needs have nothing whatever to do with the time of day, the time of night, or the day of the week. One wonders, really, why we make such a point of telling parents to put the new baby on demand schedule. He is born to that schedule, he is fully addicted to around-the-clock care; and if anything is harder for good parents than going along with the demands of his addiction, it is trying to go against them.

Finally, this totally dependent and perpetually needing infant acquires at birth the power of vocal communication. For the next four to six weeks he will use it very frequently and always negatively. His parents will get no positive vocalizing from him: he will communicate his discomforts immediately, by wailing, hiccuping, or coughing; and when he is satisfied, comfortable, and peaceful, he will be quite uncommunicative and probably sound asleep. We take this pattern so for granted that it seems strange to consider what it might do to new parents, and to the parent-child relationship, if the newborn laughed on his first breath instead of crying, and thereafter signified distress by silence, and comfort by laughter or purring. This is not merely facetious speculation, but a question: Could anything else serve so well to sensitize parents to their infant's total dependence upon them as the invariably negative quality of his early vocalizing? In any case, there can be little doubt that it adds appreciably to the parents' stress.

What they do to cope with this stress (and to keep it from draining away their surplus strength too fast) looks irrational but perhaps more than any other one thing marks them as good parents: they simply refuse to accept the fact that he communicates negatives only. They insist upon trying to obtain some positives from him. They learn to value (if you like, overvalue) every evidence that he is benefiting from their good care; they note the ounce-by-ounce increase in his weight and the lengthening intervals of his sleeping and waking. They are quick (if you like, overquick) to interpret his behavior as *personalized* nonverbal communication: when they pick him up, he "snuggles" to breast or shoulder; when they hold a finger to his hand and his fingers close around it, he is "latching on." They talk to him about these things and their pleasure in them, quite as if he could understand the words; and when eventually he seems to listen, when his eyes find the parent's face and he breaks into a smile, they know that he "recognizes" them. They are not satisfied, even then: they continue to woo him as if only their wooing could persuade his personality potential to begin little by little to unfold. They ask nothing of him except that he use their nurturance for his own needs and, to use Erikson's term (2), that he learn to trust them, to have implicit faith that they will keep on supplying all of his needs.

There are two things to be particularly noted about this earliest interpersonal relationship. In the first place, it is the probably ineffaceable ideal of our primitive dependency needs. We can repudiate it in our waking hours and whenever we feel strong and able to cope; but whenever we are really beat, sick or frightened or in despair, what we want is what the lucky infant has: someone who always perceives and supplies our needs, understands and responds to all of our nonverbal communications, delights in us, believes in us, and asks nothing of us except our implicit trust that that someone will always keep on supplying and understanding and asking nothing in return except our trust.

In the second place, this initial parent-child relationship transmits from parent to infant the beginning of the ability to relate positively to others. Assuming that the quality of any feedback is in large degree dependent upon the quality of the prior feeding into, then the deeply perceptive, unconditional altruism that flows so freely from parent to infant in these early months appears to convey the first emotional supplies to the infant, so that he acquires something with which to respond positively. The infant whose first dawning sense of well-being occurs in an interpersonal context is thereby *positioned*, as it were, toward interpersonal relationships; but positioning alone is not enough. If he is not somehow supplied with more than he has to have in order simply to survive, he can do no more than survive.

Given this initial surplus, however, the baby responds—at first, globally. He makes no distinction between parents and not-parents, he smiles at everyone who smiles at him, beamingly sure that everyone in this everloving world will take good care of him. He has become aware of Others, without yet having any awareness of himself as distinct from his world. His maturational readiness for that next step is probably evidenced by his responsiveness to Others, but it takes a new stressor to separate him and the world he lives in, to evoke in him a beginning sense of self. That stressor comes from the parents, as they begin to move toward a time schedule for him.

When they no longer pick him up at his first wail, when they no longer feed him at the very first hint that he is hungry, when they leave him alone when he doesn't want to be left alone—in all of these things his parents are exposing him to the stress of his unmet needs; and it is in this stress that he begins to feel distinct in his world. Because he has good parents, he isn't overexposed to stress, and he isn't deprived to a damaging degree; he is picked up again, he is held and fed and talked to and played with, and his faith is restored; but then he is put down again and left alone, and again feels relegated to separateness. There is a new note in his crying now, an outraged, impassioned appeal to his parents to come back, to come and get him before he exhausts himself with needing.

Gradually, out of repeated alternations of such needing and having his needs met, the baby learns to trust—specifically, to trust his parents. Note that the development of trust, as the first achievement of psychosocial growth, requires both of these two things: first, enough experience of being well loved and cared for to stimulate a strong and active desire for more of the same; and second, enough exposure to delays and disappointments to propel him into trusting as the only possible way to span those delays and disappointments. Perhaps never afterwards are we so daring in our interpersonal relationships as we are in daring to trust our parents when we are totally dependent upon them and totally unable to understand why they come and go or when they will come again. Such an act of faith must tax the homeostatic drive to its utmost, and this seems to be evidenced by the two new phenomena that usually accompany it, namely, the baby's suddenly becoming (a) fearful of all not-parents, and (b) acutely sensitive to nonverbal cues. It is as if—in order to achieve this act of faith—he must transfer onto all not-parents the greater part of the anxiety aroused in him by these first-recognized abandonments; and the anxiety that remains, that he cannot so transfer, heightens his sensitivity to his parents' moods.

The first of these new behaviors, his fearfulness of not-parents, is likely to be more pleasing to his parents than otherwise, because it highlights the baby's attachment to them. The second behavior, however, his heightened sensitivity to their moods, they will find stressful. They may know (although new parents often do not know) that it is easy to demonstrate, with any well-loved baby, that you can call him every dirty name in the book, and as long as your voice tone is gentle and caressing, he will respond happily; and, contrariwise, you can use every endearing term you can think of, but if your voice has a sharp edge, he will take fright. They may know this, and they may be able to steel themselves to his crying when that is a part of their plan of training for him; but to go in to pick him up, while thinking hard about something else, and to see his eager smile hesitate and suddenly turn into tears—this is apt not merely to reach them, but to undo them.

There is likely to follow, then, a kind of interpersonal transaction that leads to the baby's next learning, the very important learning to please. Let me move toward this by making a further point about the baby's nonverbal receptive skills at this early age. If, as I think, they are a function of his felt dependency, they will be simply either-or: either you are devoting yourself wholly and happily to him, or you are totally rejecting him. Such either-or simplicity is by no means restricted to babies; it is likely to remain at least residual in all of our significant dependency relationships. And most of us, as adults, tend to work our way out of it exactly as the baby does—not by becoming more perceptive, not by learning to distinguish between rejection on the one hand and preoccupation or headache or fatigue on the other hand, but by becoming more appealing. Who would argue for the advantage of acquiring a new interpersonal perception as against the advantage of acquiring a new interpersonal skill?

Consider, now, how a good parent will probably feel when a baby, reading the parent's face, bursts into tears. The most likely reaction, I think, will be an uprush of remorseful tenderness, a special effort to reassure and comfort, and then a special delight as the baby begins to smile again. Here is a kind of interpersonal transaction that, repeated only a few times, can begin to demonstrate to the baby that he *can* reach his parents at need, that he can secure parental attention even when it is not freely offered. You have only to watch a baby working at this to perceive how important it is to him. He will resort often to crying and clinging, but he will also instinctively try his luck at charming, patting, amusing, beguiling. He will develop a large repertory of techniques aimed at reaching his parents, and he will become remarkably accurate in discerning which ones work and which do not.

As he learns more and more surely how to please his parents, he can afford to relax his vigilance toward not-parents, can begin to relate more trustingly to them, too, *not* because they have proved themselves trustworthy, but because he has learned how to elicit attention, affection, and approval from everyone around him. It is, as a matter of fact, a most delightful period for the baby, because his learning to please is supported by all of his other learnings at the same time, his first words, his first steps alone, his beginning to feed himself, his catching on to the idea of a game. If we were to put it in Harry Stack Sullivan's terms, we might say that our small child is now luxuriating in all the rewards of feeling and being good-me (7).

But by the time the child is two years old, or thereabouts, the equilibrium of the family is again upset: again room has to be made for a new member, and room is made—now chiefly at the expense of the two-year-old. Again, as when he was first confronted with delayed gratifications, the issue is not that he is critically deprived. He has simply been *robbed*. From having had 100 percent of all available parental attention, he is suddenly cut down to having no more than half of it. His mother leaves home; his father takes care of him, but not very well and not always attentively; and when his mother comes home, she brings a new baby with her, and both parents seem to expect him to be delighted about the whole affair! Moreover, he has not only suffered a 50 percent cut in the quantity of parental attention offered to him; the quality of that attention has changed, too. Where always before he had been excitingly novel, and his parents were sensitively tuned in to him at all times, now suddenly he is no longer novel, but quite familiar and taken for granted.

Under such new stress, none of the alternatives open to him—in the "natural" or random course of events—is exactly rewarding. He can go through his whole repertory of ways to please his parents, and now win from them only a passing smile, an approving nod, or a pat on the head, before they return their attention to the new baby. He can regress and behave like the new baby, since they seem to be so pleased with that behavior: only it doesn't please them at all when it comes from *him*. Finally, when he erupts into bad-me and sets out deliberately to provoke them into paying him more attention, they discipline him for his mischief-making and forcibly restrain him in his temper tantrums. Then he subsides into depression.

And it *is* depression. We all have an ineradicable need to believe that our dependency relationships are binding contracts; in the light of that need and that belief, this child's situation is the two-year-old's equivalent of the violated marriage vow, with only the difference that no one spelled out any contract terms. Nevertheless, under the condition of his being their only child, his parents wooed him into trusting them and being happy in his dependence upon them—and then they changed the condition, broke the contract, and got themselves another baby.

(You will see here another reason for my making our hypothetical protagonist a first rather than a last or an only child. For only children and for last children the changed condition in the unformulated parent-child contract usually comes somewhat later on, and may take any of innumerable forms, and would therefore be too time-consuming to go into. For all other children the advent of the next child in the family constitutes the changed condition that offers the simplest paradigm of the basic issue.)

The direction of the child's next coping effort is determined by what the changed condition implies for him. It does not feel good to be totally trusting of people who have betrayed you once and are therefore capable of betraying you again; but neither does it work very well to be angry at people on whom you are still dependent. Therefore, of necessity, you change from being totally trusting to being conditionally trusting, and you set about to make yourself less dependent. The two things seem to occur simultaneously, but I think that an interaction process is involved, somewhat as follows.

The change in the quality of the child's trust in his parents is subtly expressed in the way he looks at them now (more doubtfully and as if across greater distance). It comes through, loud and clear, in his occasional inconsolable crying, with its unmistakable note of grief (if he is no longer always able to reach his parents with his efforts to please them, they are no longer always able to reach him with their efforts to comfort him). To allow this to go on, to be forced to recognize it fully, would be intolerably distressing; and so at this point, I suggest, the parents enter into conspiracy with the child, to plow under and out of sight all the primitive part of his dependency need.

They give him full support in his intent to become less dependent upon them, an intent that manifests itself in a marked spurt of learning. He becomes stubbornly insistent on trying to do things for himself. He responds routinely to every parental suggestion or request with an emphatic No! He leaves the house oftener, even leaves the yard; he visits the neighbors, finding a part-mother here and another there, and maybe a part-father or a part-grandfather as he ventures farther afield. If this is not entirely pleasing to his parents, at least it is better than being on the receiving end of the child's hurt and mistrustful glances; and with his making such evident strides toward self-dependence, they are not alarmed by the occasional reappearance of his primitive dependency need. They can deal with it gently, supportively, casually (and perhaps a little gratefully, too), knowing that it will not last long. Gradually, thus, they begin to grow familiar with the two-steps-forward-and-one-step-backward pattern of psychosocial growth.

What they are much slower to recognize is that in this process the child has begun to stereotype his parents, to take them for granted, and to relegate them to the background of his consciousness. The fact that he uses them when and as he needs them, which is very frequently, somehow obscures the fact that he conceives of them now not as people, but only as parents. This is an essential security measure for him as he moves into his next big task, which is to learn about people through experimenting with many different kinds of interpersonal relationships. If he were to recognize his parents as people, he would have to consider his relationship to them as also subject to experimentation; and subconsciously he knows that it would be better to forgo all experimentation than to take such a risk.

Like any healthy child, he will continue to test his parents a good deal, but that is not the kind of experimenting that he's carrying on with other people—it is rather more like the antic behavior of a puppy straining at the leash, brave in the knowledge that the leash is strong and firmly held. In a sense, the child indulges in a similar kind of antic behavior in the area of his new interpersonal operations: although he has excluded his parents from these new interpersonal ventures, he is secure in the knowledge that they are still there, keeping an eye on him, and ready at need to protect him and to help him sort out the meanings of what happens between him and his peers.

The Extended Relationships

As we watch children over the years from the preschool stage to the late adolescent or early adult stage, we see them involved in so many kinds of activities that it seems farfetched to suggest that they are centrally, or even seriously, concerned with sorting out dependencies and dependabilities. If we listen to them, however, we hear the same theme over and over again, from the four-year-old, the ten-year-old, the teen-ager, on the playground, in the classroom, and at home—the indignant, shouted accusations: "That's not fair!" "You cheated!" "You're a liar!" But over and over again in these recurrent outbursts there is ample evidence that children are deeply concerned about breaches of contract, as they perceive them.

There is ample evidence of their confusion, too, and for good cause. Long before a child enters school, he is confronted with three major sources of confusion. The first is his discovery that he can successfully trick his parents—and, by extension, that people do a lot of lying to each other and deceiving each other, and are astonishingly willing to be lied to and deceived, as long as it doesn't seem to cost them anything. When our small boy tried pinching and hitting his baby brother, he was punished; but then he discovered that if he smiled and talked love-talk to the baby, he could squeeze him as tightly as he liked, to make him cry, and his parents would only interrupt him and chide him gently, happy to assume that he was only inadvertently hurting the baby. Eventually they begin to encourage him, even to coerce him, into other dishonesties: when he has been openly defiant or disobedient, they insist on his saying that he is sorry, and they accept without question or challenge his mumbled words, even while his face is still scarlet with rage. Not infrequently he may watch them smile at departing guests, talking about what a pleasure it was to see them, and then, when the front door is closed, hear them say, "Oh, what an evening! What dreadful people!" About the only kind of sense that one can make of this sort of thing is that you'd better always do the opposite of whatever you really want to do—tell a lie if you really want to blurt out the truth, and be truthful whenever you really want to lie.

The second source of confusion also shows up when the child is still very young, when one day he approaches baby brother's crib with malevolent intent, only to have the baby look at him and break into an ecstatic smile, unmistakably delighted to see him. What is he to do when he finds himself suddenly loving and grateful toward the very same person that he most wants to hurt? This is not the first time that he has been so caught. It has happened to him before in relation to his parents, but it was too threatening there to be allowed to enter his consciousness. No similar threat being involved here with his sibling, the child finds himself entrapped in bewilderingly mixed feelings; and from here on he will be plagued by ambivalence for years to come. Because we are oddly prone to attach only negative meanings to the term *ambivalence*, we should note that by definition ambivalence includes positive as well as negative feelings. For the child here, his resentment of his sibling is fully as strong as it was before, but now it is opposed by the sudden emergence of equally strong feelings of tenderness toward him. His wish to hurt him is blocked by a wish to protect him. In short, his fiercely cherished sibling rivalry is in danger of being undermined by the beginning of a sibling alliance. (Even this term, let alone the concept, is unknown to a dismaying number of people who know a great deal about sibling rivalry!)

Ambivalence is always complex, but the underlying issue is quite simple: when you feel strong and full of leadership, you want others to depend upon you, follow you, do what you say; but when you want to be by yourself, or do something just by yourself or for yourself, you don't want any followers tagging along; and when you're in a real jam, what you want is someone that you can depend on, not a useless someone who wants to depend on you. You love people when they do what you want them to do; you hate them when they refuse to do what you want them to do; and since they insist upon doing what they want to do, instead of what you want them to do, you can only love them when their wants happen to coincide with yours, and the rest of the time you hate them. This is putting it primitively, but a small child's feelings are primitive feelings, and something of the child lingers on in all of us.

The third source of confusion is the fact that all of the child's peers are being just as ambivalent, just as changeable and unpredictable as he is in what they want, except that everybody wants to put everybody else under contract terms. The result is that in the early years of his peer relationships there is a constantly shifting and changing balance of power and dependency, an interplay of whim and impulse and resort to crude expediency—in fact, what looks very much like a random course of events. The child will make demands on his peers, and have some of his demands met and others rejected; and others will make demands on him, and without any perceptible rhyme or reason he will sometimes meet the demands and sometimes reject them. He will fight, hurting and being hurt, sometimes winning, sometimes losing. Whenever he cries or runs away, he will smart under the shouts that follow him—"Sissy!" "Crybaby!" "Scaredy-cat!"—and as often as opportunity offers he will hurl the same terms at any other child who cries or runs away. Yesterday's best friend will be today's worst enemy and tomorrow will become best friend again, without acknowledgment on the part of either child that any change was involved in the process. Both will simply be dealing with the fact that solitary playing is not very exciting for either of them, compared with playing together.

But there is learning going on through all these interactions, and as the child improves in verbal communication skills, he begins—with the help of his parents—to sort out some of the meanings of his interpersonal adven-

tures and misadventures and to recognize some of his learnings. Such learning comes slowly, cause and effect in relationships being often separated
from each other by so long an interval of time that it takes real searching to
link them together. His parents add something to his confusion, too,
because they tell him that if he wants to have dependable friends, he must
himself become dependable; that if he hopes for fair dealing and generosity
from others, he must be prepared to offer fair dealing and generosity to
others; and that if he wants his friends to value him, he must somehow
prove himself to be of value to his friends. Yet time and time again the child
can prove to his parents that his being dependable and fair did not evoke
dependability and fairness in others. His parents, being honest, will concede that this is true, but they continue to keep their approval contingent
upon his becoming dependable and fair.

Gradually, over time, and through a long series of shifting and changing alliances, of testing others and being tested by them, he begins to find
and recognize the people who, like him, are struggling to become dependable and fair, and who therefore offer the more rewarding relationships. By
the time he is nine or ten years old, he has developed an ideal of fairness in
peer relationships, an uncompromising ideal to which he commits himself
completely. This does nothing at all to resolve his ambivalent feelings,
which remain attached to whether he gets what he wants or has to forgo
what he wants at any given time. He has merely superimposed upon his
ambivalence an intellectual recognition that contracts involve a this-for-that
exchange between two people. But the intellectual recognition helps him to
inhibit the expression of his most negative reactions, and thus reduces the
likelihood of their disrupting his relationships.

The first ordering of his peer relationships is thus an attempt to effect
an exact matching of give-and-take—fairness in exchange for fairness,
dependability in exchange for dependability, and so on. The second ordering of these relationships, which may come in his friendships with
boys, but is perhaps more likely to come as he grows more interested in
girls, is based on the differences between people and the mutually en-
riching reciprocity that these differences may offer. The friend who most
often seeks his companionship may not be the companion whom he most
enjoys; but it is gratifying to be sought after, and so he gives companionship in return for (and to further encourage) being sought after. The
friend who most trusts him may not be the friend whom he most trusts;
but it feels good to be trusted, and so it becomes worthwhile for him to
be trustworthy, thus inducing his friend to continue to trust him. He no
longer has any need to restrict his relationships to people who behave

as he behaves. On the contrary, he becomes quite engrossed in looking for all kinds of differences in people, and—still experimenting—he tries relating to different people in different ways, and delights in his growing versatility and sureness in such relating.

A distinct harbinger of approaching adolescence is that the child loves to talk about his experiences. He needs to talk, he needs to be able to try out, with chosen confidants, his interpretations of what he has done and how he has felt in his interpersonal experiences, and of what other people have done and how they may have felt.

He enjoys during these years yet a third kind of interpersonal transaction, without arriving at any clear understanding of it. It appears somewhat out of place in the present context, but since it occurs quite frequently during this stage and has real import for subsequent developments, let me try to clarify. I would make a distinction between loving and liking, considering *love* to be basically need-determined and therefore often concerned with wanting the loved person to change in one way or another, so as to become more perfect to the need. *Liking*, on the other hand, values the liked person just as he is, makes no demand for change in him, asks nothing, and offers nothing except itself. Liking, so defined, has nothing to do with contract terms, with interdependencies or mutual responsibilities, with histories or futures. It is pure positive affect bonded to recognition, very pleasant to feel, and conveying a very special kind of pleasure to the recipient. We accord it less consideration than it deserves—for two reasons, I think. The first is that for as long as we are centrally concerned with contract relationships, liking tends to be a fleeting emotion, coming and going so quickly as to escape any serious attention. The second is that, because liking involves no contract terms, because in fact it seems to enter less frequently into our most important relationships than into our most casual ones, it seems somehow amoral. When a boy finds himself liking even "the wrong kind of person altogether," he feels some concern about it, enough to guard against openly acknowledging his liking. But neither of these reasons changes the two more important facts, namely, (a) that liking is a great extender of interpersonal relationships, since we can afford to like many people whom we couldn't afford to love because they are not dependable, and (b) that liking and being liked are good feelings, whenever and with whomever they occur.

Gradually, out of these varying experiences and experiments, the boy begins to form those relatively few friendships-in-depth that will give him his first clear conception of interpersonal relationships as a sustaining network. He will speak of these friends, with the unabashed honesty of adolescence, as those "for whom I would lay down my life, and who would lay down theirs for me." It is not important that some of these friendships fade in time. What is important is that the boy has discovered in himself the capacity to form such friendships and to take full pride in them.

While the child has been engrossed with all these fascinating peer inter-actions, the parent-child relationship has somehow become a parent-ado-lescent relationship—and this is a horrible transition. We oftener think of adolescence as a time of roaring rebelliousness against familial and societal controls than as a time of significant changes in dependency relationships; but when a boy finds himself physically as big as his father, and perhaps about to become even bigger, and able to pick up his mother and carry her upstairs or down—after a brief burst of exultation, his world falls apart. His parents are now no longer stereotyped. They are people again. The understanding and perceptiveness that he developed in reasonable comfort in peer relationships now floods his relationship with his parents. At best, he is embarrassed; at the worst, he is anguished and dismayed, because his parents seem to give themselves away in everything that they do or say. The terrible illumination that reveals his parents as people at the same time reveals the primitive dependency need that he had plowed under and out of sight so many years ago. So now you have it, the ambivalence exquisite: it is intolerable to the boy to realize that he is in fact still dependent upon his parents, and yet he is; and he does genuinely love them, but he feels wretchedly sorry for them much of the time, and furious with them the rest of the time. In this really outrageous bind, his hardly acquired dependabil-ity shatters.

I don't mean to imply that all of the irrational behavior and ebullient raging that we see in some adolescents is attributable to the change in their relationship with their parents. They are under a multitude of other stres-sors at the same time. But I do suggest that a large part of the turmoil experienced by adolescents is grief because they have again lost their par-ents. Two ordinary people, mere human beings full of faults and foibles, are standing where their parents stood, and this at a time when a teen-ager still needs parents—in the background.

The small child's stress response to the first loss of his parents was to invest himself thoroughly in peer relationships. The young man's stress response to the second loss of his parents is to invest himself in pursuit of one girl after another, with the ultimate although still far-off aim of finding the girl he will want to marry. It is this aim, sincerely held, no matter at what distance, that allows him gradually to reestablish his dependability, and then to acknowledge his own dependency needs: it seems all right, somehow, to be dependent on somebody if at the same time you offer that somebody your own dependability.

To say this is not to underestimate the strength of his sexual drive. But we have been much readier to talk about sexual drives than to acknowledge the persistence of any infantile dependency need into our adult years. Careful study of what we call the oedipal child suggests that his erotic feelings flow in the channel of his dependency needs, his central concern being to secure for himself not a sexual object, but protection and caretaking. For the young man, who has by now achieved a considerable degree of self-dependence, the relative strength of these two drives is reversed, and his dependency needs flow naturally into the channel of his sexual urgings. Whether he marries the first girl to whom he relates in this new kind of way, or the fifteenth girl or the twentieth, it is in these relationships that he can most comfortably and openly combine his dependency and his dependability: and doing that removes the greater part of the dreadful surcharge from his relationship with his parents.

He can then begin again—with more realism, but also with increasing tolerance and friendliness—to seek his parents in the people that they have become. We have summarized the process in our now trite saying, "The older I get, the smarter my father becomes." As soon as it no longer matters to him that they are not perfect, he discovers that his parents are really rather fine people, after all, and that he doesn't just love them, but he often likes them, too. In fact, the closer he approaches the point at which he will separate himself from his childhood home and family, to begin to establish his own home and family, the easier it becomes for him to perceive the many positives in his first family and home. Not only does he like his parents oftener and better, but he finds his younger brother becoming more and more a trusted friend and a good companion; and similarly positive feelings spread out to cover other younger siblings (not mentioned heretofore, because the most vehement feelings of sibling rivalry are likely to focus on one person primarily, on others only secondarily, and while the next younger child is not always the primary target, he is the likeliest one for that role).

It would be a mistake to assume that this greater liking for family indicates the resolution of earlier ambivalence. It is a forerunner of such resolution, but ambivalence remains attached to dependency relationships. When dependency is no longer affixed primarily to parents and siblings, neither is ambivalence. Necessarily, however, this means that our young man's relationships with girls—insofar as these carry his dependency needs—will also carry more or less ambivalence. In his testing these relationships, he is concerned with questions that he may never formulate, but certainly some of them turn on this point: Will she really be dependable if I let myself become dependent upon her? and Am I really prepared to be fully dependable if she comes to depend on me?

Eventually our young man marries, and—in this optimal history that we are developing—finds in his wife not only a good sexual partner and a good companion, but also a part-time mother to whom he can confidently turn with his needs, and a part-time child who will as confidently turn to him with hers. Assuming that both of them have entered into their contract with healthy self-dependence and considerable surplus strength, they find themselves in the beginning of their marriage rather playing these part-time parent and child roles than having to work in them. But there is an underlying seriousness in their playing the roles, an awareness that they are major items in their contract terms. And if in their verbalizing about these part-time roles they anticipate the kinds of changes that will occur when the young wife becomes pregnant, so much the better. They can then build together for the time when her dependency needs will increase and her dependability with respect to him may well decrease—and when he, therefore, must become more dependable and less dependent—if the homeostatic balance of the marriage is to be maintained.

When we considered the birth of the first child earlier, we considered only the triple stress that the new-born infant constituted for the parents. Let us consider the same events now, briefly, from the standpoint of the male parent. It is all very well to say that he must be prepared to become more dependable and less dependent when his wife becomes pregnant, but again this change does not "just happen" in the natural or random course of events. It comes only with active coping, on his part and on hers. For at least a year the integrity of the husband-wife relationship is at risk. Before they knew that she was pregnant, their fullest and most rewarding communcation was with each other; but as her pregnancy advances, she becomes more and more involved in silent, intent communication with the unborn child. The young man has no easy way of tuning in on that communication. Only if he wants very much to understand, and she wants very much to have him understand, and both of them are willing to work at it with all the communication skills at their command, can they share enough to keep him from feeling excluded and to some degree exploited.

After the baby is born, the risk is different, but not less. The young mother's dependency need may then return to normal level, but her dependability has to be channeled primarily toward care of the infant. The new arrangement begins very happily, with both parents glowing with pride and joy and absorbed in the new kind of feeling that the infant evokes from them—an unconditional caring-for that asks nothing at all in return except that the infant use it, enjoy it, and benefit from it. That feeling is time-limited. As soon as they begin to train the baby, whatever the form such training may take, they begin to make more demands of him. For years to come, they will love him always, and like him often, but never again for the duration of their parental responsibility will they be so unde-manding of him as in the first few months of his life.

This appears to be a digression from the point of risk to the integrity of the husband-wife relationship, but unless we recognize the special quality of the parents' feelings about the newborn child, it is not easy to see the hazard. For the young mother it is wonderful to be responsible only for the care of the infant, and sure in the knowledge that her husband will take care of himself and her; and since this is so happy an arrangement at the beginning, it looks temptingly like a good pattern to make permanent. If the marriage is to survive as a marriage, however, that pattern must not become permanent. The problem must be coped with, not because it is making anybody uncomfortable as yet, but because of the basic issue involved. A young man who is consigned to playing the role of father to his wife on a full-time basis can no longer be her husband in any psychologi-cally real sense of the term. At the same time, the amount of caretaking required by the infant is a new and large demand on the young mother's energies, making it quite impossible for her to resume her role as wife in exactly the way she filled it before. Something has to give; and better that the parents give jointly than that either of them attempt to do it all. By some sharing of the taking care of the child, the young husband becomes a better father, and the young mother can be a better wife.

The pattern, then, does not become permanent, but rather recurrent. With the birth of each child the cycle is repeated. Though optimally both parents become increasingly well able to absorb new responsibilities, each year of pregnancy and the early postpartum months require the man to become more dependable and less dependent, assuming more responsibility for the care of the older child or the older children until the parents together can reestablish the homeostatic balance of the family and reinforce the integrity of their marriage. My friend and colleague Kate Wallace makes the point, and it needs to be made, that there is no greater gift that parents can give to their children than the parents' own happy marriage; nothing else so surely safeguards against the spillover of a parent's unmet needs onto one or another of the children, who in such a case becomes the victim of a kind of psychological incest.

This is by no means the only kind of coping that parents have to do in the years of rearing their family. We talk enough about the financial, social, and caretaking responsibilities of parenthood to recognize these as stressors; but there are three other stressors involved that are not so visible. In the first place, we tend to forget that the beginning of the wife's first pregnancy is often the beginning of twenty to thirty years of parental responsibility. The very duration of the demand on their dependability makes it an extraordinary demand. In the second place, while children's demands for parental care and attention fluctuate and vary over time, their central demand is remarkably unvarying and tenacious: parents must always be dependable. Because good parents consider this a justified demand, they require themselves to be able and ready—on an instant's notice and at any time over a span of roughly a quarter of a century—to mobilize their resources to meet the needs of those dependent upon them.

Finally, in the third place, they are overcommitted from the day when they first become parents. They are repeatedly confronted with the need to determine priorities among the competing clamorous demands made upon them. Whether the needs involved are trivial or momentous, the decisions have to be made; and it is not merely a matter of which child is to be indulged, and which consoled if possible. It is often a matter of having to decide between a child's need and a parent's need. Parents may be better able to wait than children are, and parents often are far more willing to step aside than children are; but by the same token, such parents are far less likely than children are to insist upon their rights, even when their need is urgent. They are therefore each the more dependent upon the other to perceive the unverbalized need and to weigh its importance. They must be prepared to parent each other in such situations, and considering that this is really no more than fulfilling the explicit terms of their contract, it is odd that it should evoke so much surprise and gratitude every time it occurs, but it does. It is almost as if, in becoming parents, each had privately released the other from contract commitments for the duration of their parental responsibility, so that for either to find that the other refuses to be so released is tantamount to a reaffirmation of their marriage vows. This is only the more moving for occurring in the context of a stressful situation—a child's need competing with a parent's.

Against these stressors the parents' coping moves in two main directions. They work at developing strength and solidarity in their family by careful pacing of each child's growth and development, by promoting his self-dependence, and by cluing him in—when he is ready and able to take it—on family problems, family hopes, and family interresponsibilities. And they talk with each other, sharing their understandings and perceptions of how their children grow and change and how they differ from each other, and continuing openly to acknowledge to each other both their own dependency needs and their gratitude when the other has reached deep into his personal reserves in order to meet those needs.

This talking together sounds perhaps too simple and easy to be called coping. But it is not always easy (they do sometimes hurt and disappoint each other, and feel more inclined to sulky withdrawal than to full communication); further, it takes purposeful planning to reserve a time for talking, not merely on an emergency basis, but as *a habit of sharing;* and further still, with work it can produce new and helpful learnings about dependency relationships. For example, whenever we find ourselves involved in decision-making about whose dependency needs are most urgent, we discover (if we stop to think about it) that we ourselves have some surplus energy still available. When our own needs are overwhelming, such questions seldom occur to us; we tend neither to perceive the needs of other people, nor to recognize the cost to them when they meet our needs. In close interpersonal relationships our ability to perceive dependency needs in others tends to decrease as our own dependency needs increase. On the other hand, when we have had to reach deep into our own resources to meet someone else's needs, we discover that we can be replenished either by seeing our help turned to good advantage or even just by having our effort recognized. Sooner or later, and more telling still, we discover that we can live not too uncomfortably with our unmet needs, provided only that our significant Others recognize that we have them and accord us the right to have them. To be so understood by the people most important to us is, in itself, like healing balm to the hurting wound: the pain subsides, and the unmet need diminishes in time.

Though obviously these are strenuous and often heavily burdened years when considered from the standpoint of dependency relationships, we should not overlook two alleviating factors that make them more than merely years that deplete. The first is that we somehow acquire a remarkable amount of sustaining strength from being needed by someone whom we love. This is not to say that it costs us nothing to meet such needs, because that always costs. It is only to say that it costs us far less to give a great deal to anyone we love and therefore want to make happy, than to give just a little to someone whom we would rather reject. The second factor is that, while our dependency relationships constitute the most critical part of our interpersonal relationships, they are still only a part, not the whole (excepting those pathological situations where an insatiable dependency need, or the fear of it, invades and ruins all relationships). We should keep in mind, to give balance to our discussion, that these years are also rich in happy and rewarding interpersonal experiences. When we postulate that a man with good coping strengths can achieve a new homeostatic balance at each successive stage of his life, we are saying in effect that what he gives is somehow balanced by what he receives, not that the two are identical, but that they are somehow equivalent.

Beyond Contract Terms

Somewhere along the line, sometime in the latter half of his years of being dependable, a man experiences two changing ratios in parent-child relationships. The first change is the obvious one that comes as his children move through adolescence toward adulthood and toward the time when he will no longer be responsible for them. He is likely to discover now what completely escaped his discernment when he himself was adolescent: that as the tension (with all of its fluctuations) gradually increases between the adolescent and his family, he looks forward—with some regret and some nostalgic yearning, but also with very real relief—to the breaking of the tension, and the eruption of the adolescent out of the family and into a life of his own.

Though it looks on the surface as if all of the action here is coming from the adolescent, that is by no means the case. It involves work for the parents, over a period of perhaps some years, and usually in the familiar pattern of psychosocial growth, two steps forward and one step back. They have to recognize and begin to adapt to their adolescent's changing perception of them as people (no longer just parents), and as people remarkable only for their unfailing ability to be wrong in everything that they do or say. At the same time, they must maintain their right to be the way they are (even when in error), so that their adolescent has something firm and steadfast to push against, as he tries to establish his readiness to assume full responsibility for himself. When he does assume that responsibility, signalizing, as it were, his graduation from his essential dependency upon them, they must be prepared to give him the most generous of graduation presents—the relinquishment of their claims upon him, the termination of the old parent-child contract. Only in this way can they free him to enter into other contracts, including (they would hope) some quite different kinds of contracts with them. The parent-child relationship does not end here, where the man's sense of ongoing responsibility for his grown-up child ends, but the ambivalences in the father's feelings are finally resolved by a process of polarization. Once a man recognizes that his shaping influence on his son is terminated, he is free to think about him with no ambiguity, to say to himself or to his wife, "This I like about him, that I don't like," or "Dammit, I always hoped that he'd outgrow his messiness, but he hasn't, and maybe it's only the other side of his generosity." There are no mixed feelings in verbalizations like these, only polarized feelings.

If the changing ratio in a man's relationship with his son presents problems to be coped with, the changing ratio in his relationship with his aging father presents equally difficult problems, and is apt to be more disconcerting by far. Perhaps it can most intelligibly be put this way: Many of us lose our parents three times before they die: first when we have to share them with a younger sibling; again, when our stereotype fails us, and we see them as people; and again, when in their aging they begin to turn toward us as toward parents. The stereotype that carries the primitive dependency needs dies hard—more accurately, never dies: the wish for a parent is a lifelong wish. Even when our parents consciously and thoughtfully emancipate us as we become adult, we tend to evaluate this, as they do, in terms only of their making no further claims upon us, not at all in terms of our making no further claims upon them. Parents, practically by definition, should be the people who are always there, in the background, but available, dependable, ready to help or comfort or counsel, able to fill in the gaps.

The point, therefore, at which it begins to grow clear that our parents are asking us to emancipate them from their old parental obligations becomes a point of stress even for the forty- or fifty-year-old man or woman (6). If we are honest, we have to admit that we go through some odd operations aimed at dodging the issue before we can bring ourselves to face it. A frequent first reaction is alarm, a quick jump to the conclusion that there must have been a series of little strokes, causing brain damage. If not this, then the old man may be just malingering, taking the easy way out of responsibility. There must at least be some oncoming senility, because he is growing forgetful, he confuses names, even the names of his own grandchildren, his mind wanders at times, and he seems to grow more and more easily moved to tears.

It is the old basic issue: simply who owes whom the right to be dependent, and for how long, and who owes whom the obligation to be dependable, and for how long?

Beyond a man's deep entrenchment in his own life situation, his orientation to fulfilling his responsibilities toward his wife and children, there are still other reasons for his finding it so difficult to imagine that an aging parent (alone now, let us say) may be realistically recognizing and accepting the fact that in the field of his parental obligations he has reached retirement age. It is somehow outrageous to think of being a parent to one's own parent, unless he is really like a child again and needing to be treated like a child; in which case you would have to add that he is an unlooked-for, unplanned-for, and essentially unwelcome child—and this is too hard a thing to say. But the only alternative is to admit that the old man's wanting to retire from dependability somehow presages his death, and in that case, consenting to his retirement becomes not only a way of compassionating, but also a way of grieving.

Yet a man who has enjoyed his father's friendship for many years does not lose the habits of friendship suddenly. He finds himself often still talking with his father as he used to talk, and being listened to in much the same way as before, with alert interest and evident enjoyment. Being thus forced to evaluate the situation more thoughtfully, he realizes that it is not peculiar to old age alone to be forgetful, to confuse people's names, or to have wandering thoughts. It may even occur to him that if most of one's other activities are curtailed, and there is nothing to distract one from thinking and feeling, then one's thoughts and feelings are likely to have peculiar immediacy and intensity. When at length he recognizes that his father is really quite undemanding, and that it is his own needs, and not his father's, that are causing him such sharp distress, it finally becomes possible for him to relinquish his claims upon his father and to begin to relate to him with that particular and poignant gentleness of the parent toward a child who has not many years to live.

What this can accomplish is one of the most unexpected developments in the natural history of dependency relationships. A man discovers in this changed father-son relationship what his children had discovered long before, in the grandchild-grandparent relationship—that old people, so released and cared for, have an enormous capacity for unconditional liking and appreciation, pure positive affect bonded to recognition and completely free of judgments and evaluations. It is the bright and clear (and usually nonverbal) communication of this kind of feeling that constitutes, it seems to me, the "graceful" part of growing old gracefully. If this is true, then it follows that we cannot grow old gracefully by ourselves, in solo performance. We can still, without anybody's caring for us or caring whether we live or die, grow old in dignity and self-containment, communicating only (in silent absorption) with our remembered significant Others; but we grow old gracefully only with the consent and presence of some (at least one) of our significant Others, the people who can most easily release and receive our unconditional liking.

This next-to-last transition in the crucial dependency relationships so far anticipates the last of the learning tasks that there is little more to add; but that is not to say that there is little further coping to do. When you have spent most of a long lifetime in first learning to be and then in being dependable, and have based much of your self-respect on this achievement, you will inevitably come under stress again when you realize that you no longer have the reserves of energy with which to meet the dependency needs of others. And when for most of your life you have been fully committed to the ideal of fairness and reciprocity in interpersonal contracts, the issue confronting you then is unequivocal: if you can no longer offer dependability, you may not make any further claims upon the dependability of others. This in itself need not constitute a crisis, and will not constitute one if our significant Others permit us to retire from active service in the field of dependency relationships, and thus free us to feel and to communicate that unconditional liking that we can experience then as serene enjoying.

The last bind comes when we find ourselves (as some of us will) no longer able to take care of even our own physical needs. To speak of one's needs and discomforts is in effect to make claim upon others for caretaking or caring attention, which seems unfair; but to deny that one has any needs and discomforts is to falsify communication and thus terminate any meaningful relationship with other people, in effect to reject them. There may be other ways to deal with this dilemma than the one way that I have seen, but having seen very different kinds of people intuitively taking this way, I think it may be the only way. The matter can be simply put. If one communicates one's needs and discomforts only in nonverbal ways, then the message reaches only the people who care enough to be tuned in to such nonverbal communication, who then give or try to give the relieving care; and then one can thank them openly, verbally (or if speech is impaired or gone, by the unmistakable look of gratefulness), not just for the caretaking, but—more importantly—also for the perceptiveness that saw the unverbalized need.

It can be thus simply put, but to handle the matter in this way frequently, let alone regularly, and perhaps over a period of many weeks, clearly requires a very high order of personal discipline, and long training in the most delicate and sensitive ways of relating oneself to other people. I have not, up to this point, attempted to demonstrate that the accomplishment of each successive change in dependency relationships is dependent upon the successful accomplishment of the preceding change, and I am not prepared to do it now; but to my eyes this final achievement has the look of the culminating event of a long and graduated series of intensive interpersonal learnings. It may not always be that, but it is difficult to conceive that it could ever be the result of just letting nature take its course.

There are a number of other pertinent things that I have not done here. For one, after calling good interpersonal relationships a sustaining network, I have offered little to show how they sustain or even that they sustain us during stress, focusing rather on trying to show what kinds of coping efforts must go into the formation of the network.

For another, I have largely disregarded the question of whether there is a critical period for each of these learning tasks, a time at which the individual is most ready for that particular kind of learning, and after which he can learn it only with difficulty, if he can learn it at all. A more immediately pertinent point is an obvious one—that any learning comes more easily if it doesn't involve unlearning something else at the same time.

For still another, I have given very little attention to the consequences that ensue when we fail to cope effectively with any of the transitional crises in our dependency relationships. But our professional literature abounds with descriptions of such failures and with detailed analysis of how they occurred. The failures are not to be ignored, but I want to fit them into the context that we have been using throughout this discussion, taking an acknowledged risk of oversimplifying in doing so.

Our networks of interpersonal relationships can ensnare us if we do not understand clearly what is involved in the crucial dependency relationships, or if our interferences in the natural and random course of events are motivated by anxiety: because whatever its ostensible aims may be, the overriding aim of all anxiety is simply to reduce anxiety—in other words, to act on the basis of what is inside us, oblivious to what is in the world outside. (Incidentally, the anxiety-motivated interferences, while they may surprise the person who carries them out, are clinically quite predictable and almost always negative in their outcomes.)

If we were always to be on the giving end of our interpersonal transactions, we could expect only to be exploited and eventually depleted. If we were to try to insist upon being always on the receiving end of them, we could expect sooner or later to find ourselves alone in the net. Another alternative would be simply to avoid forming any significant interpersonal relationships whatsoever—turning instead toward what Meehl calls *interpersonal aversiveness* and views as one of the four source-traits of schizophrenia (4). In our urban societies we are sidling in that direction: practically all of the landmark events in interpersonal living are institutionalized. Mothers have their babies in hospitals, while fathers sit together in waiting rooms. People go to church to be married, or to a justice's office, and spend their honeymoons in motels or hotels or winter or summer resorts. They go to court to be divorced. Sick people are hospitalized, and old people are sent to nursing homes. Dying people are sent to hospitals, there to die, thence to be transported to funeral homes. These outs allow us to seclude ourselves from intimate acquaintance with the naked feelings of fear and pain and grief, and obscure the meaning of the impulse that underlies our consenting to them, an impulse that looks very much like flight into depersonalization. Institutions serve a purpose, but one questions why we capitulate to them so thoroughly as we do. Are our pain-barriers so low, and our loves so weak, that we cannot tolerate the emergency emotions that are part of every enduring interpersonal bond (5)?

It is for these reasons that I have chosen the one remaining alternative of trying to search out more accurate information about what goes into the making of good interpersonal relationships, trying to break through our amassed clichés and stereotypes and socially approved but frequently unwarranted assumptions about them, and trying to look as honestly and searchingly as possible at common experiences in them. The process is highly personal, and sometimes painfully so; but it offers us at least an opportunity to interfere at those times and in those ways most apt to help us achieve a desired and "otherwise improbable outcome" (1). In the field of interpersonal relationships the most natural and probable outcomes are mistrust, rage, hostility, irresponsibility and cheating, frustration, bitterness, and ultimate loneliness. The improbable outcomes are trust, fair dealing, dependability, understanding, generosity, full empathy, and ultimate undemandingness and liking, plus the enduring relationships that these elicit and support. But if we are lucky enough to be born free of impairment and to welcoming parents who can give us that initial surplus that more and more clearly seems to be the source of all subsequent psychosocial growth (3), then the improbable outcomes are not at all impossible outcomes. They merely don't "just happen" by chance.

Chapter 3. ABOUT MIRRORS, IMAGES, AND THE SELF

When you consider that each of us is fated to spend an entire lifetime with one particular person—namely, oneself, it is astonishing that we put so little focused thought and effort into trying to make of that person someone that we can be content to live with.

Granted, we talk a good deal about the importance of self-respect. The term sounds somewhat virtuous, but we are willing to accord the virtue if it has been bought at the price of some self-denial or self-sacrifice. If the virtue is simply claimed, at no cost to the claimant, we tend to consider it not self-respect, but mere self-righteousness. Similarly, we concede the right to act in self-defense, but we scorn any self-protectiveness that goes perceptibly beyond self-defense. We encourage self-awareness (assuming that it will balance positives with an equal weight of negatives), but we damn self-absorption. We admire the self-educated, but we ridicule and, if possible, unseat the self-appointed. We approve of self-dependence, but self-conquest we view with reverence and awe.

In an unabridged dictionary there are well over a thousand words that are hyphenated with self, and this kind of moral flavor clings to almost all of them, often with intriguingly subtle nuances. Obviously, we are very much concerned about our selves, but obviously, also, we are about as conflicted, ambivalent, and full of equivocation in our attitudes toward self as it is possible to be. We are fixated, morally, at the level of ten-year-olds, uncannily quick to see and attack everything that resembles self-love in other people, and remarkably skilled in demolishing it. Recall the ringing derision of playground cries ("Ya, look who loves himself! Look who thinks he's great!"), and the quieter but merciless comments of little girls ("Leave her alone, kids. She likes herself so much, let her have herself—

who else would want her?''). Under such attacks children quickly learn to dissemble and deny any positive feelings that they may have about themselves. They do more than that: they buy, without question, their peer group's primitive belief that love is like money: whatever amount of it one holds for oneself is precisely the amount that one is withholding from others.

The underlying problem, both for the ten-year-olds who attack openly and for us adults with our conflicted attitudes, stems from the fact that human beings are both individual and social. As individuals, we all want as much as we can get; and therefore, as social beings, we all feel threatened by the greed and the power of every other individual. The ten-year-olds perceive the issue simply as a power struggle. We adults formulate it with more sophistication, as a need to establish a workable balance between what we want to demand for ourselves and what society demands of us; but we recognize, at least tacitly, that such a "workable balance" is likely to be whatever the particular individual or the particular society can get by with. We are beginning to recognize some of the dangers involved in the issue— for example, that just as society is a threat to the individual who seizes too much power for himself, so the individual is a threat to the society that tries to keep him subjugated and powerless. Whether the society involved is a nation or a state or a classroom or a family, we are beginning to understand that the principle holds: it takes strong and healthy individuals to make a strong and healthy society. The deprived, the underprivileged, the sick, the disabled—all of the presumably powerless individuals are costly drains on a society's resources. And we are beginning to become duly concerned about these dangers.

We are still missing the essential point, however, which is that positive feelings are not like money. If I give you five dollars, you are five dollars richer, and I am five dollars poorer. But if I give you liking, encouragement, admiration, I lose nothing whatsoever, even though you may gain by my giving. Positive feelings belong in that category of special resources that Glidewell defines as those that we can give unreservedly to others and still maintain intact within ourselves (10). Often they have a still more remarkable generative quality: if my liking you adds to your sense of well-being, then you are better able to like others, who in turn will feel better for being liked and will thereby be readier to like others, and so on.

Take this, if you will, as one anchor point for our discussion of self-esteem—that we are better able to develop positive feelings toward others when we feel reasonably good about ourselves. We have another anchor point in the large and steadily increasing mass of clinical evidence and a convincing and also increasing amount of research evidence that seem to link social and educational failures (8, 17, 18, 25, 29), mental illness (2, 16, 33), and delinquency and crime (4, 23, 26) to poor self-esteem. From these two anchor points we can move profitably, it seems to me, in one direction only, and that is toward learning (a) how to develop our own self-esteem, so that each of us can live more contentedly with our own lifelong, inescapable companion, and (b) how to promote the development of self-esteem in others, so that we can build a better society for all of us.

A first requirement is to define what we mean by *self-esteem,* and what we do not mean. We do not mean mere self-acceptance (as one of my co-workers in our research investigation put it, "A happy little moron could be fully self-accepting—more pleased with himself than a brighter child might be"). And we don't mean self-concept, which may be either good or poor, may command esteem or be quite powerless to evoke it. If we begin with the term itself, it is immediately apparent that it has both a denotative and a connotative meaning. *Esteem* has the same root as the verb, *to estimate*—that is, to appraise, to evaluate; so that the denotative meaning of *self-esteem* is self-appraisal, an attempt to determine the real worth (great or little) of the self. The connotative meaning of the term, however, is distinctly positive, attributing real value to the self. To conceive of self-esteem as a psychosocial resource requires combining these two meanings to define it as a *reasonably accurate and realistic appraisal of the self, resulting in the finding that that self has worth.*

It is no easy task for any of us to be at one and the same time the appraiser and the appraised, even if we agree that appraisal makes no claim to be exactness. In suggesting that we have to work with mirrors and images in the process of appraising ourselves, I am taking my cue from a beautiful piece of experimental work done by Drs. Lilli and Leopold Hofstatter and their colleagues at the St. Louis State Training School (15). Their subjects were children so severely retarded (IQ < 20) that they had never learned to talk, had never even learned to distinguish one person from another. One at a time, but four times a week for six months, the children were put into a small room lined with mirrors except for the door. Left alone there, each child slowly began to notice his mirrored images. Here were things that moved every time that he moved. When he reached out to touch one of them, it reached out its hand to touch his. There must have been baffling oddities: for example, he couldn't with his hand touch any part of any image except its mirrored hand; if he tried to touch its face, its hand would move to stop his hand, and if he tried to touch its toes, again the hand would be there. But if he put his fingers in his mouth, so would the image; and if he moved toward it, it would move toward him, until they could stand forehead to cold forehead, knees to cold knees, toes to cold toes; and if he kissed it, it kissed him. It moved beside him, wherever he went, and gradually he began to relate to it, to play with it, experimenting with its peculiar ways of play.

For each of these children who went to the mirrored room, there was a matched control child who went into a room without mirrors. Before and after each period in these rooms, all of the subjects, both experimentals and controls, were gently mothered and called by name, shown enlarged photographs of themselves and other children, and the circle, square, and triangle of the Cattell formboard. A child's progress could thus be measured if he learned to recognize his own picture, respond to his own name, smile volitionally at the experimenter, correctly place the Cattell forms on the board, verbalize at some level, and so forth, for fourteen measures in all. Not only did the children in the mirrored room enjoy being there (while the other children could not tolerate the control room for long without growing restless and unhappy), but they also averaged gains on ten of the fourteen measures at the end of the six-month training period (while the control children showed gains on only two measures). Two out of three of the children who had the mirrored room experience learned to talk intelligibly!

For all of us, as for those children, mirrors and the images they reflect are necessary to the development of that clear sense of self without which it is impossible to develop self-esteem, in the sense in which I use the term. What we become, and to what extent we become what we want to become, involves a long, slow growth process, bringing with it many vicissitudes and demanding a lot of coping; but it also involves, more specifically, our giving due regard to the image in the mirrors available to us. Those mirrors are as multiple as the people who relate to us, and to whom we relate; as our fears and anxieties, as well as our hopes and wishes; as our memories and our dreams, and as what we produce and what we possess and what we barter or borrow or give away. Not even in the clearest of the mirrors is the image exactly the same as the person that it reflects; and let us note that, since many of our mirrors are other people, with their own needs and biases and tendencies to project, the image that we see in some mirrors may bear no recognizable likeness to any self-image that we have seen before. Nevertheless, there are available to most of us mirrors enough, and mirrors clear enough, to help us learn to know ourselves if we can learn to look into them with seeing eyes. These mirrors can give us that feedback that enables us—if we want—to reshape our behavior and thus gradually to change ourselves toward becoming more nearly the kind of person we want to be.

Before I begin to discuss the major components of the self-system, as I conceive of them, one more acknowledgment should be made: much of this material is still speculative and intended more to challenge than to persuade or convince. Except for the earliest and the latest components, there seems no reason to presuppose a regularly ordered sequence in their emergence into active functioning. I suspect that the sequence may vary from person to person, and the range of years covered by such variation may be quite wide, and that further variation may result from the possibility that in some people one or more than one component will never emerge. There is fair reason to think, however, that all of the basic components of the self-system may emerge and become fully operant in many people long before they attain physical adulthood, and I am therefore going to discuss them with primary focus on the childhood years. I should perhaps warn that the names by which we identifiy some of the components sound very primitive at first; but I would add that the ultimate sophistication is the return to the primitive, with only the difference that now it is recognized as the primitive.

The Images in the Parents' Eyes

A sense of self develops only in the matrix of significant interpersonal relationships. I suggested earlier that the infant whose first dawning sense of well-being occurs in an interpersonal context is thereby positioned, as it were, toward interpersonal relationships. But a dawning sense of well-being is not the same thing as a sense of self. In the first weeks of life the infant simply absorbs all the tenderness and loving care that his parents can give him, and only gradually—in a diffuse and global way—becomes responsive to them as they minister to his needs. In describing the behavior of welcoming parents with their infant, I said that they continued to woo him as if only their wooing could persuade his personality potential to begin little by little to unfold. It is not really an "as if" matter (5). It *is* the parents' wooing of him, together with their ability to enhance his sense of well-being, that draws him into the first and indispensable interpersonal relationship, indispensable not only because it lays a firm foundation for the development of all later significant relationships, but also because it provides the infant with the security that he needs for his emergence as an individual. The baby's initial responsiveness to his parents seems purely instinctual; he learns to recognize them as the source of supplies that make him feel good, but there is nothing in this "recognition" to suggest that he has any feeling of being separate and distinct from them.

It is only as they begin to move toward a time schedule for him, exposing him to brief delays before they come to meet his needs, that he begins to perceive them as apart from him. When we discussed this same situation before, we were concerned with its interpersonal aspects; here we are concerned with its intrapersonal significance. In the times of being exposed, even briefly, to the stress of his unmet needs, the baby begins to feel distinct and separate from his world: and he cries not just because he is hurting with hunger or is wet and cold, but also because he is suddenly terrified to find himself alone.

In the emergence of the sense of self from the all-surrounding not-self, there are two odd and interesting twists. First, the pain and discomfort of the baby's unmet needs, which constitute the stressor precipitating the emergence of the self, are produced by the parents, but felt only in their *absence,* not in their presence. The baby cannot, therefore, associate these unpleasant feelings with his parents. But second, since his pain and discomfort have to be lodged somewhere, I suggest that the baby can lodge it only with the not-self, or, to use Sullivan's term, with not-me (30). In a later formulation, Sullivan defined the not-me as "that which is related to the personified self in the sense of its contradictory" (31). The formlessness that the infant was born into, and could rest comfortably in, as long as he had no sense of self, may be the source of later dark and awful horror as he experiences more and more clearly the sense of self (11).

Of course, not even this first and global sense of self takes shape suddenly. The only relatively sudden thing about it is the immediacy with which it establishes its absolute supremacy in its small host. All of the rest is gradual learning, progression by way of repeated alternations of rest and thrust, of the baby's experiencing stress from time to time, and in between times sleeping well or lying peacefully awake, bemused by moving lights and shadows or by his own hands or his voice (21). It seems reasonable to assume that in his earliest times of experiencing the sense of self and the stress of unmet needs, the baby does not know what it is that he wants. He simply wants; it is only as his parents repeatedly reappear and meet his needs that he begins to develop some glimmering perception of *what* he wants; and that is now not just his parents' presence in the room. It is no longer enough for him to recognize his parents, or even to anticipate that, now that they have returned, they will take care of him. Once he has acquired the sense of self, what becomes crucially important to the baby is *that his parents recognize him.*

The new development comes through clearly in the different sounds of his crying. While at times he still sounds like an infant giving voice to physiological tensions, at other times his cry is unmistakably the sharp wail of fright at finding himself alone; and if you go in then to pick him up, he will cling tightly for a moment or two, and then pull back until he can see your face and search your eyes—not just to be sure that he recognizes you, but with real urgency to make sure that you recognize him. His embryonic sense of self is not up to coping alone with the dreadful, all-surrounding, waiting nothingness of the not-me; he cries out for rescue of that most precious self—and finds rescue in his parents' recognition of him.

This is his first mirror, and he will need to see himself in his parents' eyes over and over and over again as he struggles to secure himself out of his earlier formlessness. It takes a long time. The threatening aspect of the not-me remains starkly clear in the reaction of the three-year-old when a familiar adult "teases" him by pretending not to know him. Such teasing will incite a child to clamorous protest verging on sheer panic and continuing until even an insensitive adult repents the game. (The threatening aspect does not vanish with childhood, although we learn ways of keeping it at a distance. It remains in the fear of death; and for that matter many an adult, going under an anesthetic, experiences a devastating sense of loss as his sense of self is washed helplessly out into the not-me.)

Thus, the first differentiation of the self-system is the emergence of the self out of the not-self. But if we are going to trace an optimal development, I shall have to add a modifier to that statement. For the lucky infant whose parents delight in him as he is and as he grows and responds and learns, the first self-image that he sees in his parents' eyes is in fact good-me, and this will be the only self-image that he will see reflected in his parents' eyes through all of his first year and well into his second year of life. All of his learnings will be fun-learnings, both pleasing his parents and flowing naturally into his expanding and pleasurable sense of self, so that good-me will have considerable content long before the *concept* of good-me takes shape.

But that halcyon time does not last indefinitely. Sooner or later good parents must induct their small child into the socialization process, which means that he must learn to give up certain gratifications, must learn to control certain impulses—must, in short, begin to learn the not-fun kinds of learning. This precipitates the second differentiation, the division of the self into good-me and bad-me—and it comes as a terrible jolt to the baby to see bad-me clearly mirrored in his parents' stern and disapproving eyes. Anyone who has watched it happen, who has heard the parents' first sharp "No!" or has seen the first light slap on the hand, will remember the baby's look of astonishment and dismay, usually followed by outraged tears, with a tinge of heartbreak: this is because now it is clearly and unmistakably his parents who are inflicting the bad feelings on him. The same mirror that let him experience self as good-me, lovable, valuable, adorable, now shows him bad-me, not lovable and not adorable (though still valuable *because* he can learn).

Regrettable as it may seem at first blush from the viewpoint of the baby and often of his parents as well, the sense of bad-me is a social necessity, an essential ingredient of psychosocial growth. But a baby doesn't know about social necessities and psychosocial growth. Having enjoyed being a baby, doing exactly as he pleased and always being wrapped in his parents' warm love and approval, he simply wants to perpetuate his babyhood. Learning not to wet or soil whenever or wherever he pleases, not to strike out whenever he is enraged, not to grab for everything that he wants—these are stressful learnings for the small child, and he will not engage with stress if he can avoid it. He wants to have his own way. He wants his freedom, and he wants to enlarge his freedom, not limit it, and if he is a sturdy child, he will rebel vigorously against any attempt to limit it.

What his parents have to do, therefore, is to make it more unpleasant for the child to refuse to engage with stress than to get with it. And there is only one way in which they can accomplish this: that is by using the full potency of their relationship with the child, who is still completely dependent upon them, to coerce him into learning the not-fun kinds of learning. They have to put their own weight into the balance, they have to position themselves in such a way as to persuade and (if you like) to propel him into coping efforts. If, up until this time, they have given him only smiles and praise and encouragement, then their withholding these and substituting frowns and reprimands, instead, will constitute a stress more painful to the child than coming to grips with the issue before him, the whatever-it-is that he doesn't want to learn. It can be argued that the child would learn more readily and at less cost if his parents simply ignored his bad behavior and reinforced only the good; but this would not eliminate bad-me. Bad-me would still take shape in the child's mind from the parents' sometimes giving and sometimes withholding praise and encouragement. At least to a sensitive child the difference between plus and zero is just as clear, if not as great, as the difference between plus and minus.

It is more to the point, I think, to remember that parents are people with deep involvement in the parent-child relationship, so that socializing their child is about as stressful for them as for the child. If at times they speak sharply to him or lightly slap him on the hands or the seat, it is not

entirely unnatural and conceivably not entirely bad. In saying this I do not
for a minute mean to condone what we commonly call corporal punishment, which by now has taken on all the strength of an operational principle as lacking in intelligence as it is in human decency. But parents who are
not so filled with anger that they have to be fearful of losing control are not
going to abuse a child, no matter how far he provokes them; and the child
who is old enough to *understand* the initial "No!" and has chosen not to
heed it is also old enough to understand, accept, and learn from the quick
and unmistakable parental reaction. It conveys clearly to him that what he
does or does not do is a matter of importance to his parents, and this carries
its own particular kind of reassurance to the child, even though he may
never recognize it as supportive.

Let me take this a step further, in an effort to sharpen the point. There
comes a time, when the child is older, when the wiser strategy is to ignore
the negatives and reinforce only the positives (and we shall be dealing with
that later); but in these very early years, when a child's self-esteem is still so
weak and vulnerable a thing, it is a greater kindness and a much more positive help to let him resolve his frustration and rage in the security of the
parent-child relationship than to leave it to him to resolve them (or swallow
them) as best he can by himself.

Even so, a healthy child will not learn quickly to "come to heel" whenever he sees his parents frown. The probabilities are that he will rebel
repeatedly over a whole multitude of issues for as long as he lives in his
parents' home. But the later rebellions serve a different end from the earlier
ones that we are considering now, which have to set the foundation of self-
esteem. Not until the child has had the experience of seeing himself in his
parents' eyes as bad-me, and then by his own coping efforts has successfully
reestablished himself as good-me, does he have the beginning of a means of
self-appraisal. There is no way for him to evaluate "good" except by contrast with "bad" or at least with "not so good." But a very significant portion of whatever self-esteem we possess derives not from what we have
actually done, but from all of the worse things that we might have done but
did not do! Just as the private knowledge of our wrongdoings leaves us feeling guilty, there is the other kind of private knowledge of all the times
when we could have cheated but didn't, that makes us feel good.

For the child to find himself restored to his good-me, once again clearly
lovable in his parent's eyes, and by virtue of his own coping efforts, gives
him some sense of worth, but not enough. The esteem of his parents is of
great importance to him, but it is not the same thing as self-esteem; and it
is largely if not entirely up to the parents to transform the one thing into

the other, by giving the child full and explicit credit for his successful coping efforts. This point, called to my attention years ago by Dr. Felice Emery, is one that I should like to make as strongly as I can, because it is so easily overlooked. We tend to assume that a child will know that he can take credit to himself when he has turned in a good performance; but this is an unwarranted assumption. When parents have used the power of the parent-child relationship to persuade the child to engage with stress in order to grow by coping, the most natural thing for them to do is to leave the credit in the relationship—to say things like "Mummy is so proud of you!" or "That's the kind of little boy that Daddy likes!" The only message that comes through clearly to the child in such remarks is that the parent is pleased because the child has performed for the parent. This may be enough to keep the child motivated to learn, often for many years, but it adds precious little to his strength and self-confidence. Instead, it makes him only the more dependent on his parents, by binding his self-esteem to their approval.

Here again, then, we need some interference with the "natural" course of events, in order that some "otherwise improbable outcome" can be achieved—in this case, that the credit is returned to the child himself, so that it adds to his self-esteem. The interference strategy is simple enough: the parents need only refrain from saying what comes most naturally to tongue, and say, instead, things like "Good boy! you did it!" or "Well, now *that's* earning the right to feel pretty good about yourself!" Since comparable comments continue to be gratifying to all of us throughout our lives, as every thoughtful person knows, there can really be only one difficulty involved—the fact that we are all so eager to take credit wherever we can find it that we often forget to give credit where credit is due.

The essential point to be made about these first components of the self-system is that they are parent-determined and parent-bound. Both good-me and bad-me belong to the parents more than they belong to the child, just as—at this early age—the child himself belongs more to the parents than to himself. (Not-me belongs to nobody, which is its dreadfulness.) But the implications of this essential point are several and highly significant.

In the first place, we have clear evidence that parents (or parent-substitutes) are indispensable to the psychological development of their young. Many investigators have contributed to the evidence, but to mention only two, there is the work of René Spitz with human infants (27, 28), and the work of Harry Harlow and his colleagues with baby monkeys (12, 13). Spitz's infants, receiving adequate hospital care, but inadequate or no mothering, developed what he has called "anaclitic depression," often terminating in early death. One group of Harlow's monkeys, who were separated from their mothers at birth and raised during the first year of life in complete isolation, became grossly defective adults with psychotic behavior, even though they had received the best of physical care. Another group of baby monkeys had wire or cloth mother-surrogates triggered to violent shaking when the babies clung to them; and this group also became seriously defective, unable to learn or to relate, the males incompetent to mate, and the females harshly refusing to mother. Apparently it is a critical need in infants, both primate and human, to have parents in whose recognizing eyes the babies can find an image of themselves, and whose comforting responsiveness gives to that image the look of good-me. Lacking that when they first and most urgently need it, they become—oftener than not, perhaps—completely unable to use it when it is later offered to them. The image in the parents' eyes is thus not merely the first of our self-images, but is the one without which there apparently can never be another.

The second implication derives more from clinical evidence and logic than from empirical data (at least, to my knowledge). Unless the baby's sense of good-me has been well established before he is exposed to the noxious feelings of bad-me, he is caught in a vicious trap. It is terribly easy to get stuck with bad-me when that has been one's most frequent experience; and if a child's primary self-image is bad-me, then the direction of his subsequent development is almost certain to lead to social inadequacy, or delinquency and crime. There is one escape easy to come by, and that is to yield to the regressive suction of the not-me, to go back into the darkness and formlessness of the not-self; but this is the path to psychosis. If a child is to grow up healthy, it is imperative that his first two years bring him abundantly the feelings of being good-me (24).

The third implication relates to the importance of these parent-determined images in effecting linkage between a child's learning and his developing self-esteem. It will be obvious that in one degree or another these images transmit a considerable part of the parents' value system to the child, the image of good-me being shaped by what the parents love or like or need or enjoy, and the image of bad-me shaped by what they fear and condemn and reject. In the Freudian formulation (6) these two images together, when they have become internalized, constitute the conscience. It is perhaps not so obvious that these images are not always clear and stable and cleanly demarcated from each other; but consider what must happen if father and mother have differing value systems and cannot resolve their differences, or if their value systems are shifting, equivocal, or uncertain. If they have differing value systems, the child will receive one kind of message from his father, and a quite different kind of message from his mother; and if their value systems are unstable or unclear, the child will receive one kind of unclear message at one time, and another kind of unclear message at another time. In either case, his images of good-me and bad-me will be muddy and confused, his conscience will be uncertain and conflicted, and he will have nothing to help him to learn.

The process that is optimally involved closely parallels that by which the baby learns to trust his parents. For that earlier learning, if you remember, two kinds of experience were required: first, enough experience of being well loved and cared for to stimulate a strong and active desire for more of the same; and second, enough exposure to delays and disappointments to propel him into trusting as the only possible way of spanning those delays and disappointments. In a similar way the child's development of a valid and valued self-concept, which ultimately will enable him to develop trust in himself, requires that he have two kinds of experience: first, a clear enough sense of himself as good-me to stimulate in him an active desire for more of the same; and second, and later, a clear enough perception of himself as bad-me to propel him into learning how to circumscribe and control the behaviors that evoke the negative image, while increasing his repertory of skills to evoke the positive image. Only in that way is the child's early learning securely rooted in the interpersonal network, in the human and humanizing relationships that are most significant to him. This is socialized learning, and is likely to continue as such, feeding into the child's self-esteem.

What we need to recognize is that children can and do learn in other ways without such parental help, and by their learning they add to their power; but unsocialized learning serves the aims *only* of pleasure and power, and recognizes no law except the primacy of the child's own needs and desires.

One further step is essential to effecting the linkage between learning and self-esteem. Although the early learning should be rooted in the interpersonal network, it must then be allowed to grow freely *beyond* the parent-child relationship; again, this requires that the parents give the child full credit for having learned, so that (a) he can add the credit to his self-esteem, and (b) his learning becomes his own, no longer bound to the parent-determined images. He is not *driven* to learn because that seems to him to be the only sure way to hold on to his parents' esteem. Granted that sometimes this is a child's distorted perception of his parents' basic attitude, nevertheless distorted perceptions can warp and stultify growth just as surely as overdemanding parental attitudes can do; we have all too many children who dare not stop, who cannot rest, who must keep on achieving because they feel of no value except as they achieve.

And so it takes two deliberate actions on the parents' part, one after the other, to effect the productive linkage between the child's learning and his self-esteem: first, their use of themselves to motivate him to learn, and then their leaving with him the credit for learning. Once these two things are done, the child is free to begin to seek self-images that will belong to him, not just to his parents.

The Observer

Somewhere along the line, and often in very early childhood, there emerges in many of us the most peculiar component of the self-system, a character that I call the Observer. When I term him (*him* genderless) peculiar, I mean both that he is odd and that he is singularly personal—odd in that he seems to be so disengaged a part of the self, and singularly personal in that no one else can ever see or hear him. "To each his own" is the phrase that describes his most salient characteristic. For each of us our Observer is exclusively and uniquely our own mirror. I regret the cryptic quality of these initial statements, but the subject that we have to deal with here eludes easy description. I shall have to go around and about, considering him now in this aspect and now in that, hoping that at some point in the process we can catch a clear glimpse of him.

To begin with, while I am inclined to believe that every psychologically healthy person has his Observer, and in some degree feels and reacts to his influence, many otherwise well-put-together people manage to remain unconscious of his existence. His status in the self-system is much like that of the jester in the king's court, some hundreds of years ago: he is an impudently objective and exasperatingly incorruptible eyewitness of our behavior and some of its more disconcerting implications, but he can be easily ignored or—if not that—ostracized. The pertinence of his comments about other people is often entertaining and sometimes very helpfully sagacious. The pertinence of his comments about us more often seems impertinence, sheer cheekiness, amusing enough if we are in a good humor anyhow, but otherwise intolerable.

It is this characteristic in him, I think, that accounts for the curious similarities in the terms that different people use to describe their own Observers. A former patient told me that she had "a little imp that sits behind my eyes, between my ears, and never misses one damn goofy or pretentious thing I do." A psychiatrist friend speaks of his as "that joker in the back of my head, who watches me hamming around, and says, 'Add a few tears, and you'll maybe fool even yourself—but you don't fool me.' " A very small child that I know says, "I didn't see me do it, honest!" and then adds softly, "but the Little Me inside me always sees."

My own Observer, as I recall first conceiving of him, was elfin and not inside me, but somewhere just behind and above my left shoulder, from which vantage point he was able to see—all at the same time—(a) my behavior, (b) my illusions about my behavior, and (c) the incredibly simple and naïve me so revealed in the behavior and so duped by the illusions. Just at first I was fascinated at seeing myself in that mirror, and full of admiration for my Observer's powers of discernment, but I quickly became indignant and defensive—which got me nowhere, of course, because the more I protested and made excuses, the more my Observer grinned, completely unassailable in his I-know-what-I-know assurance.

Without venturing to guess how typical these four descriptions may be, I infer from their anthropomorphic quality that the Observer emerges quite early in the lives of some of us. If it came later, in adolescence or in adulthood, this component of the self-system would more likely be spoken of as "memory" or "visual recall" or "an autocritical bent" or—with Miller and his colleagues (19)—"the observing function of the ego." Adults are not likely to visualize a little imp sitting behind their eyes, or a joker in the back of their heads, or an elf stationed behind their shoulders, unless they are harking back to some indelible fancy of early childhood.

We can only speculate about what precipitates the emergence of the Observer, but my speculations run something like this: We know that the small child delights in playing peek-a-boo. Even before he can walk alone, he can learn—sitting on his father's lap—to hide his eyes behind his hands while Father says, "Where's Johnny?" and then suddenly move his hands aside to uncover a beaming face as Father exclaims, "*There's* Johnny!" Out of such games, as time goes on, he begins to gain a sense of identity as Johnny, including a dawning consciousness of being Johnny even when his parents don't see him—when, for example, he is hidden behind the chair.

Then one day, and perhaps almost by accident, he extends the game still further, goes into a room when no one else is there, and squeezes himself into the corner behind a chair. Lying there alone, maybe hearing his parents talking together in the next room while he does nothing more than watch the dust motes drift through a ray of sunshine, the peculiar thing happens: suddenly *he seems to see himself* lying there, very still, and knowing what nobody else knows, not even his parents—namely, where he is

and how it feels to be there. Part of him has become his Observer, giving
him the first self-image that belongs to him alone. And he exults in it,
quietly—A. A. Milne has captured the feeling in one of his poems for (and
about) children, although he relates it to bedtime, duties done and fond
adults gone, closing the door behind them, and then:

> So—here I am in the dark alone,
>   There's nobody here to see;
>   I think to myself,
>   I play to myself,
> And nobody knows what I say to myself;
>   Here I am in the dark alone,
>   What is it going to be?
> I can think whatever I like to think,
> I can play whatever I like to play,
> I can laugh whatever I like to laugh,
>   There's nobody here but me (20).

Notice that it is no longer good-me or bad-me; it is clearly now my-own-
me, and that is its special deep thrill.

But notice also that Milne's child is somewhat older than our small
boy: the lines suggest not a first experience, but a familiar and cherished
pleasure, without any insecurity. The first experience may well bring with
it some insecurity, I think, a pang of separation anxiety: go back to our
small boy still lying there behind the chair, and suppose that his parents call him, and he doesn't answer and doesn't move. In knowing where
he is, when his parents do not know, he is likely to experience a new,
half wonderful, half terrifying sense of separateness from them—and
as if a flashbulb had gone off and a picture had been taken, he sees himself
with unforgettable clarity. And he has acquired the beginning of conscious
memory. Even if at first he cannot tolerate his separateness for more than a
few seconds before he has to call out and run back to his parents, he can
now at will (and sometimes willy-nilly, too) see himself as he was then,
lying there behind the chair, knowing what nobody else knew then or need
ever know. Later on, his ability to see himself will not be limited to present
or past experience, but will extend into the future. That, however, does not
concern his Observer, who deals only with the present and the past.

When I first began with these speculations, years ago, I thought that it
took some such moment or moments of stillness and disengagement, of
heightened sentience without concurrent interpersonal involvement, to

produce the Observer. I still think it is easier to describe his emergence in this way, but I no longer think that it is the only way in which it can occur. I suspect that any time of heightened sentience that is accompanied by even a fleeting wish for disengagement from interpersonal involvement would give him opportunity enough to emerge and make his observations and comments. If this is true, he must serve as a homeostatic mechanism, and, as such, we should expect him to be welcome at all times. And yet every one of the four descriptions that I gave earlier, of my patient's Observer, of my psychiatrist friend's, of my little grandniece's, and of my own, conveyed quite clearly a feeling of being attacked or at least of being unfairly spied upon.

The fault, I think, is in us, not in our Observers. We should prefer to see ourselves as always good and admirable, possessed of all virtues, and pure of all vices; and our Observers pay no attention at all to what we should prefer. They are completely reality-oriented, and the realities that they reflect to us include not only our environments and the way we look in our environments, but also the telltale breakthroughs of our unconscious motivations, the needs and wishes that we would rather not acknowledge, the aims and intents that we would rather keep suppressed. That persistent neutrality, that bland disregard of good and bad and any other *values,* is part of why our Observers infuriate us so often. They neither blame nor approve, and in this respect they are critically different from Montaigne's "invisible censor within," whose blame, in Virgina Woolf's interpretation (35), is the more to be dreaded "because he knows the truth; nor is there anything sweeter than the chime of his approval." Montaigne's "invisible censor within" sounds very like that one of Sullivan's "supervisory personalities" whom he calls his "reader" and describes like this:

> I have been very much interested in the character of my reader, never quite interested enough to conduct an extended investigation to discover his actual origin; but enough to know that he is a charming pill, practically entirely responsible for the fact that I almost never publish anything. He is bitterly paranoid, a very brilliant thinker, and at the same time an extraordinarily wrong-headed imbecile (30).

These are both valid concepts, bearing on the fact that for any verbally skillful person it is treacherously easy to be eloquent, and very, very difficult to be honest and accurate; and they both make use of the Observer: but the Observer really has no truck with their censuring or supervising.

The exasperating thing about the Observer, as I see it, is that he is simply an information-seeker who will not confine himself to turning up just the information we want, but proceeds instead to turn up a lot of information that we don't want at all. He will show us ourselves looking piteously vulnerable when we want most to look self-sufficient and strong; and he is just as likely to show us ourselves looking perfectly strong and self-sufficient while soliciting or enjoying sympathy and help from people around us. And so the collisions that occur between us and our Observer, while they are numerous and often painful, are not the result of any attack, of any movement whatsoever on the part of our Observer: they result simply from our own insistent attempts to seduce our Observer into buying our pretensions—and our Observer is not to be seduced. We want him to show us that what is in the world around us is congruent with what is in our heads, particularly with respect to the way that we ourselves look or sound or act; and he mirrors all manner of other images, instead. They are by no means all disagreeable images. Many of them are as innocent as that of the small child in the corner behind the chair, watching the dust motes drift through a ray of sunshine, or as seeing oneself in any remembered time of enjoyment or good performance. They are disagreeable only when they are completely at variance with what we want to see.

But if we are eventually to achieve some degree of congruence between what we really are and what we want to be, then we have to make use of our Observer's observations. In no other way can we approximate more and more closely that "reasonably accurate and realistic appraisal of the self" that is the necessary base of self-esteem. If we discard his findings as either irrelevant or unacceptable, our sense of self remains no more than a series of shifting and changing images, forever dependent on mirrors outside of us. We shall do well to cultivate his acquaintance, because—although sometimes he turns up uninvited—he is really not at all attention-demanding. Most of us can remember a lot of times when we have been either so preoccupied or so engulfed in strong emotion that we remained oblivious to things happening right before our eyes. This kind of experience is common and normal, even in people on intimate terms with their Observers. It is only the steadfast refusal to look into one's own mirror that leads to living without learning, without remembering, and without becoming able in part to foresee.

Anything, therefore, that delays or precludes the emergence of the Observer in a child should be of grave concern to all of us who work with people; and two such things occur commonly enough to deserve attention. The first is that kind of constitutional hyperactivity that prevents a child from ever disengaging himself or finding any seclusion except in sleep. When a child cannot stop experiencing long enough to learn from experience, he learns only by conditioning, and he remains bound and confined to the parent-determined images of good-me and bad-me. In addition, his motor-drivenness and often his overreactivity, as well, make him so difficult to deal with that he provokes more and more annoyance and hostility in the people around him, so that the mirrored images he sees are more and more often bad-me, and less and less often good-me. Now, happily for some (and for many more of them soon, we hope), ways have been found to break into that vicious circle so that these children need not be trapped into feeling forever bad-me. Special education facilities, sharply reducing the amount of stimulation to which the children are subjected, perhaps offer one method of treatment; but we have seen some children effectively helped in regular classrooms, when teacher and parents and physician worked closely together to achieve alleviation of the condition through medication, and then *to seize the opportunities thus afforded to give the child some more favorable experiences in interpersonal relationships, in learning tasks, and in moments of disengagement in which he can begin to see himself in a happier light.*

The other kind of concerning situation is subtler, but more difficult to remedy. If a small child is disciplined by being put into isolation before he has had the experience of finding pleasure in seclusion, it can almost be taken for granted that he will be psychologically disadvantaged, if not disabled. To any small child, to be isolated for misbehavior is to be rejected for misbehavior, and the pain of feeling rejected is too enormous to leave room for any new learning.

We tend as adults to feel both baffled and provoked to anger when, to discipline him, we have sent a child alone to his own room and then discover ten minutes later that he is playing happily there by himself. And yet what do *we* do when we have a troubling problem to work through and need to communicate with our Observer in the process? We are likely to work over the problem while playing the piano or washing windows or waxing and polishing the car or even watching TV. The activity serves our need for security while we are trying to sort out what exactly it is that we have to cope with and how we might best begin to cope. The child's apparently happy play serves him in the same way. It is more thoughtful play than happy play; it enables him to tolerate the pain of feeling rejected while he learns—*so that he can learn*—from the experience: and this is possible only for the child who has had some previous experience of enjoyable seclusion, has acquired his own Observer, and has begun to use him as a mirror.

For those to whom this Observer personification may seem meaningless or merely fanciful, let me try to summarize in somewhat more scientific terminology. In all of us a stream of feelings, impulses, and drives goes on all the time on two different levels, a conscious level and an unconscious one. Both levels influence our behavior, and affect the way in which we relate to our environments. Most of us have, also, a feedback mechanism that informs us (with varying degrees of accuracy) about how our environment in turn affects our behavior. From that feed-back we can, if we choose, tease out some understanding of which effects are due to conscious processes in us and which are due to unconscious processes; with this kind of understanding we can modify our behavior and determine our course of action in ways that will allow us to move more smoothly and directly toward our goals (34).

The Ego-Ideal

As good-me and bad-me constitute a natural pair, so perhaps do the Observer and the ego-ideal. The function of the former pair is to promote the child's growth through motivating him to engage with stress; the function of the latter pair is to give direction to his growth by clarifying for him—in hours and instants of disengagement from stress—the differences between what he is, in his own perception, and what he wants to become.

While we usually think of the ego-ideal as belonging to the world of our daydreams (or if you prefer, to the world of our ambitions and aspirations), it is nevertheless firmly secured to the realities of our lives and shaped by them. For example, long before the small child conceives any wish to be different in any respect from what he is right now, today, he will be replicating certain of his parents' behaviors, not—at first—because he is trying to be like his parents, but simply because certain physical, constitutional determinants make those behaviors natural for him. The little boy who inherits his mother's type of skeletal framework and muscular overlay is likely to develop a gait, a stance, a set of the head or the shoulders more like his mother's than his father's. The same sort of inborn, inherited factors can result in a child's more resembling a great uncle or a grandfather whom he has never seen than either of his parents, whom he sees daily or hourly. While conscious and continuing efforts over some considerable period of time may modify these likenesses, the child's constitutional endowment is inevitably going to make it easier for him to change in some ways than in others.

But this is not the only way in which such factors can affect a child's early identifications with other people. If he hears too often in childhood that he is like enough to this or that relative to be that relative's child, then he will to some degree identify himself with that relative, and his regard for himself will to some degree reflect the kind of regard accorded to that relative. When the relative is regarded with affection or admiration, the child benefits by being identified with him; but when the relative is regarded negatively, either in whole or just in part, the child is all too liable to feel alienated and disadvantaged by the identification. Small children cannot readily distinguish between an objectionable person and an objectionable trait in an otherwise acceptable person. They see things as either-or, holistically. In addition, until the sense of self is firmly established, a child has little choice except to take it that he is in fact whatever his adults say he is. Here, then, is one of the great dangers of embittered conjugal relationships or hostile in-law attitudes: in whatever way or ways the child resembles one of the embittered parties, in just such way or ways he tends to alienate the other embittered party. Unless the adults involved are aware of the danger and in control of their own emotions and behaviors, the child may suffer a seriously impaired interpersonal relationship of great importance to him, and a warping of every ego-ideal that he might develop. He is not free to dream just any dream of how he would like to be, because it has already been fixed for him that in certain respects over which he has no control he is always going to be like somebody else.

Within these limiting conditions, however, children have a remarkable capacity for imitation, and they use this capacity to "try on for size" certain behaviors that they have observed in the people close to them. Here the child neatly turns the tables on his parents. His earliest concepts of himself, as good-me and bad-me, reflect the way he sees himself in his parents' eyes. Now, as he begins to imitate them, his behavior faithfully mirrors the way his parents appear in the child's eyes—and as any perceptive parent can tell you, such imitative behavior can be at times highly disconcerting, realistic but far from flattering. Obviously, the child's Observer does not just observe the child himself; he observes the parents as well, with the same dispassionate, rigorously reality-oriented eyes.

Now the more exactly a child can imitate another person, the more closely the child's feelings and attitudes really resemble those of the imitated person. Imitation is not often, if ever, merely superficial. *As long as the self-concept remains susceptible to shaping influences,* then "to act like" tends to resonate into "to feel like." In the context of acting out our feelings, discharging our emotions into behavior, we are familiar with the linkage of the psychic-emotional system to the physical-behavioral system.

We are less familiar with that linkage when the flow is in the opposite direction—that is, from a given kind of action to its analogue in feelings; but this is the path by which we achieve our identifications with other people. First we act like them, and then we begin to feel like them. This is the essence of the process of actualizing this or that part of our ego-ideals.

We give so much attention to the importance of the little boy identifying with his father, and the little girl identifying with her mother, that we tend to forget that there are two other, earlier, and therefore weightier bases than sex for a child's identification with a parent. These are love and power. A child does not need to be old enough to be aware of being sexually like one parent and unlike the other before he can understand quite fully that his parents are, for him, the main source of love and power. Underlying the child's every imitation of his parents' behavior is a compelling, enduring drive to gain for himself as much as he possibly can of love and power.

The character of the child's early sex identification, then, whether it is appropriate, inappropriate, or mixed, will be determined in large part by whether it is the parent of like sex or the parent of unlike sex who offers him the most attractive model of lovingness or powerfulness or both. It has to be said that the little boy who sees his mother as more worthy of emulation than his father, and the little girl who sees only her father as worth emulating, her mother not at all—these children do have problems, sometimes with far-reaching implications. But it should be said, also, that the damage to self-esteem, which is so often associated with inappropriate sex identification, is a culturally inflicted damage serving no good purpose. The early sex identification is not so fixed and unchangeable a thing as a child's first image of himself as good-me or bad-me; it is subject to change and modification and even reversal, *unless* the significant people around him close the door on change. They can do this. By making a fetish of our stereotypes of "pure male" and "pure female" they can glue the child's early sex identification to his image of good-me or bad-me, as the case may be, and thereby make the one as nearly impossible to change as the other.

We will be more realistic, as well as more helpful to the people we live with and work with, when we do away with those stereotypes and begin to understand what Freud has said plainly, that psychologically we are most of us more bisexual than we commonly recognize (7). Someone (and I'm not sure who) has said that the optimal condition is for men to be about four parts male to three parts female, and for women to be about four parts female to three parts male. This is difference enough to allow for complementarity without sacrifice of congeniality, to promote singularity without endangering partnership, and to provide—for the lucky child—parents in both of whom he can see a blend of lovingness and powerfulness, so that he can happily identify with both. (My conviction about this was briefly shaken, I confess, by the appearance of "hippies" on our national scene. I am troubled when I see two people and cannot tell at first glance if they are both male or both female or one of each sex. But their apparent need to look bisexual is certainly no more troubling than the men who dare not be gentle, and the women who dare not be strong.)

Nevertheless, the stereotypes are with us, to the point where, as Caldwell has pointed out (3), we cannot simply study "the socialization of children;" we must study "the socialization of boys" and "the socialization of girls." Not until we understand clearly the cultural forces that impinge so differentially on boys and on girls will we be able to modify them effectively enough to produce happier, healthier men and women, better marriages, and more positive parent-child relationships.

While the earliest ego-ideal, the child's identification with one or the other or both of his parents, is shaped by a largely inarticulate, unconscious process, the later ego-ideals of the child, of the adolescent, and of the adult must become conscious and articulate if they are to serve to guide psychosocial growth. You have to have a pretty clear idea of the kind of person you want to become before you can start to work constructively to become that kind of person. If, for example, it is part of my ego-ideal to have many friends, I will neither just sit and wait for them to come my way, nor focus my efforts on trying to prove that I am a superior person and therefore deserve friends. Instead, I will study earnestly the people I know who have many friends, try to discern what it is about them that attracts so many others to them, and then set about to develop as best I can the same traits in myself.

But how many of us, who work with children or live with them, ever think to help them clarify for themselves what kind of person each wants to become? We ask them often enough what they want to be when they grow up, and we expect the kind of answers that they give: "a cowboy," "a dancer," " a spaceman," "a mother." The question is of no help to a child, nor do we in asking it have any real intention of being helpful; and the brevity with which most children answer and then dismiss the matter says that they recognize it for the idle palaver that it is.

We can and must do better than this, but we need to be sensitive to the risk that is involved. In its formative phases the ego-ideal is not only a constantly changing part of the self-system; it is also a very fragile part. It can often be shattered by the merest touch of discouragement or ridicule. When someone says, "I really wanted to be a concert pianist, but my talent didn't quite come up to that level," we can listen without great discomfort because the speaker is obviously quoting his realistic Observer. Similarly, when someone says, "I wanted to be a surgeon, because I was good with my hands, but there wasn't any money to help me through college, and so I'm a hairdresser—still with good hands," we glimpse the realistic Observer in the background. It is quite something else to hear someone say: "Well, I wanted to be a lawyer, but my Junior High counselor said that I wasn't college material, and my old man never risks money on a poor bet, and so that was that," or "I thought at least I could grow up to act and talk like a lady, if I worked at it, but my father and brother always said I was just a goon, and I just couldn't keep on fighting that."

These are gratuitous cripplings, whether they stem from unbridled hostility or merely from ignorance and insensitivity. They occur with appalling frequency, and they are most devastating when they come from people whom we admire or trust or love. If we are not to be despoilers, we must recognize both the fragility and the importance of the ego-ideal, and be surely enough in control of our own behavior to see a child "try on for size" a role too big for him, without needing at once to "cut him down to size." There simply is no adequate substitute or compensation for a shattered ego-ideal. There is nothing that can excuse the adult who discourages or ridicules a child. I doubt that it would be overstating the case to say that when the ego-ideal is shattered, the growing part of the personality is finished, and only the reactive part is left.

The fact remains that if the ego-ideal is to become a purposeful and hard-working part of the self-system, gradually but steadily bringing direction and order into the child's psychological growth, it must become a clear image in the child's mind. More accurately, it must be a series of clear images, each one more finely differentiated than the one before. When the small child acquires his first hero, he admires him globally: a hero can do no wrong, just as a villain can do no right. But most children, by the time they are of school age (and many children well before that time), have begun to differentiate between the admirable and the not-so-admirable in even the people whom they most admire. They are ready then to be helped to think in terms of *what kinds of traits* they most admire in other people and would like to develop in themselves. They can learn to talk about the ideal father, the ideal mother, the ideal teacher, the ideal friend, and each of these formulated ideals will be a mirror in which they can see the image of some part of what they want to become. They can, in short, begin to envision themselves in the future.

We had a game, when I was a fifteen-year-old, a very serious game shared only with closest friends. Each of us wrote a letter to herself or himself at age twenty-one, describing as explicitly as we could the kind of person we hoped we would have become by then. That is a long time ago now, but I still remember vividly the astonishment we felt six years later, when three of us reread and shared those letters, and found that we were in fact well on the way to becoming the kinds of persons we had hoped to become. It is a never-ending process, since by definition the ego-ideal can never be fully actualized; and at each step along the way we pay a price, because we have to choose between alternatives, one of which necessarily has to be foregone. Nevertheless, each step toward the actualization of the ego-ideal adds something of significance to our self-esteem.

Specifically-Me

Between good-me and bad-me, the Observer and the ego-ideal, our small child now has four monitors of his psychosocial growth; but before he can gain a sure sense of self, he has to have something more than these. That something I call, by extending the Sullivan kind of terminology, the specifically-me.

From early on, he has a strong drive that keeps him working at this particular task. Having enjoyed the experience of being engrossingly interesting and delightful to his parents, there is nothing that he wants more than to keep on enjoying that experience. But even if he is not confronted with a new sibling rival who seems more engrossingly interesting to his parents than he now seems—even if he is an "only" or "a last," parents do in the course of time become accustomed to his face and to his ways, so that he loses much of his sense of being novel and special and unique. In addition, parental focus on training a child interferes in varying degrees with their enjoying him. The result is that at some point in time he receives much less of this particular kind of gratification than he wants. And it is partly in the hope of finding more that he ventures afield, visiting other homes in the neighborhood, searching for someone, child or adult, who will look at him with interested eyes and be eager to get acquainted with him.

To become in some way or ways unique and especially attractive is not always easy, and to be in one attribute or another unfailingly interesting is of course impossible; and yet both of these are among the cardinal (if unacknowledged) goals of all of us. The sense of being specifically-me is an essential part of self-esteem; but it takes a lot of images and a lot of mirrors, and a lot of learning about which mirrors reflect truly and which images

are worth perpetuating, to give form and content and stability to the concept of specifically-me.

Through the years of fast-growing, from childhood to adolescence, not
even the image in a plain glass mirror is a very stable one. It is an important one, and given opportunity a child can spend long periods of time looking at himself, smiling, frowning, turning his back and bending over and
looking between his legs to see his head and face upside down, gesturing,
posturing, trying to become familiar with all the ways he can look, and
with the ways in which he changes, as when he first loses a tooth or gets a
new kind of haircut or suddenly seems to be growing very big ears. In fact,
just about the time he becomes familiar with how he looks, his looks change
again, and he has to start the process all over. It takes a lot of looking into
the mirror to keep himself informed about himself.

There is, happily, much more stability in the images of himself related
to the things that he can do, because these *accumulate* rather than merely
change. When he learns to go up and down the steps, alternating the left
foot and the right, he becomes securely Johnny-who-can-go-up-and-down-
steps-just-like-a-grown-up. When he learns to dress himself, to get the right
shoe on the right foot, to get into his pants, and to get on his T-shirt right
side to, he is quite securely Johnny-who-can-dress-himself-by-himself. As
he learns to ride a trike and throw a ball and turn a somersault, he is well
on his way to becoming Johnny-who-can-do-a-lot-of-things. Anything and
everything that he learns to do adds solid content to his concept of specifically-me, and helps to balance off the confusingly changing images of himself reflected to him in the recognition of other people.

These images *are* confusing. While at four years old he is still, with his
parents, a little boy, with his two-year-old brother he is big and powerful
and sometimes fierce. With his friend two doors away he is the boss, but
with the two big guys down at the corner he is just a scared rabbit. How
can you tell what your size really is, when you feel so small if you're with
big people, and so big if you're with smaller people? And how can you tell
how brave you really are, when your being a bully or being a coward
depends simply on whom you are with at the time?

It is this state of affairs that gives us reason to speak of school entry as a
crisis in the child's life—a crisis in which his first teacher plays a crucial
role. While children differ widely in the degree of their vulnerability, they
are nevertheless all of them highly vulnerable at the point of school entry,
as they move onto their first formal social testing ground. In the sturdiest of
them, the pride and excitement that they feel in the morning as they leave
home to embark on this new venture evaporate when they find themselves

in the classroom, surrounded by twenty or thirty or forty other children, most if not all of them new and strange. Their uncertainty about themselves mounts high, along with their uncertainty about their classmates. Usually their teacher also is new and strange to them; but children know that, psychologically as well as physically, water flows downhill, and so they know at least one thing about their teacher—that she is stronger and more powerful than they are. If, therefore, they are in need of more strength and security and protection than they have within themselves, it is to her that they must look for the additional supply.

Here I want to digress again at some length, to consider how teachers are implicated, not only in the development of a child's self-esteem (which they hear often enough), but also in the child's struggle to establish his specifically-me. Let us grant, right off, that most teachers will have some anxiety of their own to cope with in the first few days of school. They will be concerned to lay down quickly and clearly the ground rules for classroom behavior, and to develop as soon as possible the most effective groupings of children for this kind of activity and for that. They may have to deal with a child, and sometimes with more than one, who is really panicked by being separated from home and mother; and if they are lucky enough to have none of these, but are sensitive to children, they will still be aware that here and there in the room sits a shy child who will need an extra measure of encouragement. Facing part or all of this, it would be far more comfortable for a teacher not to recognize that all of the other children, the stronger ones who are ready and eager to learn, are sitting braced and hyperalerted through at least the first day, and often through the first week, and that in their hyperalertedness and hypersensitivity everything that the teacher says and does (whether encouraging or discouraging, permitting or limiting) is magnified ten to twenty times in the children's perceptions. A reprimand aimed at one child may intimidate twenty or thirty others, and even the failure to notice one child's distress may be interpreted as rejecting coldness by many or all of his classmates.

I should be hesitant to make a point of this magnification of all that the teacher says and does, if it merely increased teacher-anxiety. Fortunately, however, we have in a small but fine study reported by Harris and her colleagues (14) not only documentation of the teacher's potency with small children, but also a straightforward directive as to how she can use her potency constructively. The experimenters in that study observed the child's behavior and a teacher's responsive behavior long enough to obtain a stable picture of the strength of the response; and then they asked the teacher to reverse her mode of response—in other words, to ignore that particular behavior in the child, and to respond only to the opposite kind of behavior. When the teachers did so, the result was a significant weakening of the first kind of behavior, with a concomitant strengthening of the second kind until it became well established. Then the teachers were asked to return to their first mode of response, and when they did, the child's first kind of behavior was reestablished. And yet once again the teachers were asked to reverse their patterns of response, and did so, and again the children's behavior changed accordingly. The same kind of result was obtained for all of the teacher-child pairs, even though the initial behaviors of the children varied widely.

Here is ample evidence of the teacher's potency. But I have omitted two salient points—first, that the children's initial behavior was of an undesirable kind, and second, that the teachers responded to it in the way that comes most naturally, by focusing on the undesirable behavior and trying (usually in very supportive ways) to encourage the child to change it: and *the chief effect of the attention and the encouragement was to reinforce in the child the behavior that elicited them in the first place.*

If the findings of this study are generalizable, and subsequent reports indicate that they are, it is not the teacher's intention but her attention that is important to the small child, and he will continue, as part of his drive to establish his own specifically-me, whatever kind of behavior best elicits her attention, regardless of whether it meets with her approval or not. Baer and Wolf make the further salient point (1) that the teacher of very young children cannot choose *not* to shape their behavior: her only choice, whether she makes it deliberately or by default, rests in *how* she will shape it. Sometime, I hope, we shall have curriculum planning that will give the teachers of young children a week or two at the start of each school year to focus primarily (which is not to say *entirely*) on searching out and rewarding with her recognition and attention some positive behavior in each child, ignoring as far as possible the undesirable behaviors, reinforcing the desirable behaviors—as it were, handing to each child a small package of her esteem that he can add to his self-esteem.

But the stresses and strains of a child's first days in school do not end with the first days. They can be greatly diminished if he can become happy and comfortable in the classroom; but kindergartners are lowest on the totem pole of school, and whatever pride a child may have felt in being big enough to go to school, and however much of that pride he can maintain by making a good adjustment to the classroom situation, he learns quickly that kindergartners are the runts of the whole school, the smallest, the dumbest —if not the overlooked, then at best the looked-down-on. Everybody else is older and bigger and smarter. There is only one thing that can solace him for such mortification; and that is adding day by day, to the content of his specifically-me, new learnings and new achievements and the rewarding recognition of his teacher for these.

Here we need to consider what we call the "invisible" children, the ones whom you don't notice when they're present, and don't miss when they're absent, whom you can't remember clearly when you can't see them, whom you never can call by name or whom you call by the wrong name altogether (and can you think of anything else so small that adds so much to the specifically-me as being positively known and identified by your own name?)—in short, these are the children who seem to be merely part of the furnishings of the room.

Our attempt to study these invisible children has not been notably successful, but we quickly discovered that invisibility is often only in the eye of the beholder. A child who is invisible to one person may be perfectly clear to another. Then we realized that some children have high visibility, positive or negative, by some circumstance over which they have no control. A child who is conspicuously large or conspicuously small, relative to age and sex, a child who is strikingly beautiful or memorably homely, or who has bright red hair or a crippled foot or any other congenital, inherited, or early acquired characteristic that sets him noticeably apart from his fellows —such a child has visibility whether he likes it or not.

We finally recognized that it might be more accurate to speak of "high visibility" and "low visibility" than of "invisibility," if we wanted to refer to the person observed rather than to the person observing, because there is good evidence that people can learn skill in observing. We had in our study one very alert teacher, with something like thirty years of experience, and a fine ability to individualize the children in her class. At the end of the first day of school she was able—without reference to her class roster—to write down the names of twenty-three of the twenty-eight children in her class, along with a phrase denoting what she saw as his chief asset and his chief liability, and to estimate whether he would be in the upper, the middle, or the lower third of the class in academic achievement as measured by achievement tests toward the end of the year. (Interestingly, eight of those more visible children performed better than she predicted they would, while four out of five of the less visible ones performed at a lower level than she predicted. This raises an intriguing question that we cannot yet answer: Is high visibility a correlate of good performance, or is a teacher more effective with the children whom she sees most clearly?)

For our highly skilled and perceptive casework observers, who were not

allowed to interact with the children, a few children remained relatively
invisible over the three years of the study. Some appeared to have fallen
naturally or to have learned very early to move into a pattern of accommodating to stress with minimal change. They seemed to function almost
pseudopodially, as if sensing the locus of stress well before they touched it,
and sort of flowing slowly away from it into some safer, more comfortable
position. Their passive-adaptive movements were so gentle and slight and
fluid as to be imperceptible—except that over a period of time one would
find them occupying a space different from the one they had occupied
before. In the narrowest possible sense of the term they are well adjusted,
so extremely well adjusted that there is no clear difference between them
and the space they occupy. What happens to these children as they grow up
we don't know; we assume that it will be determined in part by their luck
and in part by how much intelligence they can call into the service of their
comfort. Conceivably, with enough luck and enough shrewdness, they
might reach adulthood without mishap, still sitting it out, like the man in
Voltaire's tale, who—facing execution for theft—successfully bargained
with the king for a year's reprieve by promising that within the year's time
he would teach the king's pet ass to sing. To his rational friends who said
that this was folly, he replied: "A year is a year, and in that length of time
the king may die, or I may die, or the ass may die, or the ass just might
sing!" Note that he indicates no intention to try to teach the ass to sing—
he merely proposes to sit out the time, growing only as to dimensions of the
rump. We suspect that some of our invisible children have that same attitude.

Others, however, and they are the reason for this long digression, we
think may be invisible simply because nobody yet has seen them as individuals, has looked at them with eyes that recognized something different and
unique in each of them, has listened to them in a way that invites them to
come out of their backgrounds, to stand forth and be identified, to become
known. We hypothesize that they have had no close and continuing, meaningful one-to-one relationship to provide a springboard for the development
of the specifically-me. They have had no experience in the kind of interpersonal intimacy that allows for their developing interpersonal skills. They
are not "shy," as we commonly mean that word, because shyness is perfectly visible and always includes—along with whatever else it may
embrace—a heightened awareness of others and of self. Glidewell's term
socially inept (9) fits them better.

But they are not doomed to remain invisible if a perceptive teacher spots
them and can find and reflect to each an image that is somehow distinc-
tively and specifically his own. That is the first and also the easier part of

the task of rescuing such children. Having gone unnoticed for five years or more, they are starved for recognition, and they will attach themselves gently but irremovably to anyone who notices them and thereby in their own perception claims them. They don't know any other way to respond to interest, and can never be fully satisfied, but stay too long, and return too soon and too often, always appealing, always needing. It takes great patience to keep one's interactions with them on a positive level, and I think we should not expect teachers to do the job without a lot of help from other people, but teachers are in a better position than anyone else to spot these little waifs and begin the rescue effort.

For teachers at all grade levels it should be noted that with the formation of each new class, with the assignment to each new teacher, the child sees himself in many new mirrors. He has to renew his search for the image of the specifically-me, and he does this by jockeying for position with his classmates and his teacher, acting out and testing out, until he has found and secured the place he wants in the social structure of the classroom, or—as happens to the less confident and less visible children—settles into the lower positions. Don't overlook the fact that all children, as they enter junior high and again as they enter high school, find themselves again at the bottom of the totem pole, the youngest, the dumbest, and the looked-down-on by everyone else in those schools, and this right after having been—the year before—the oldest, the smartest, and the looked-up-to. Small wonder that these two changes are also crisis points!

These early days are hard on teachers, but it can be of some help simply to understand what is going on, and to know that usually the matter is soon settled: the social structure of a classroom is quickly formed, and—once established—has remarkable stability for the rest of the school year (8), except as the teacher herself may effect change through her interactions with her students. So much for teachers in the context of the specifically-me.

Because the search for this component of the self-system is a lifelong search, it is intriguing to speculate on what is really operating when the child enters that stage where, to judge by his behavior, the most important thing of all to him is to act and dress and talk and be exactly like his friends. Why, if the specifically-me is critically important to growth toward self-esteem, does it seem normally to go underground for a period of years? An obvious answer is that in the widening world of puberty and adolescence anxiety increases, and one way of binding anxiety is banding together with others who are equally anxious. But I think that something more than this is involved, in somewhat the following way.

In the process of becoming socialized, we find that we usually have to give in order to be given to, whether of love, approval, esteem, or any other psychological goods. By giving our fullest approval to the people most like ourselves, we stand a good chance of accomplishing two things: gaining their approval in return, and partially (consensually) validating our own worth. Two people are stronger than one, and if to secure the strength of another to add to our own we have to go through a series of small modifications (I becoming more like you in some respect, while you become more like me in another), we become both more alike and stronger. Three people are stronger than two, and four people are stronger than three, and at some point in this process our self-validating group becomes strong enough to assert and maintain its own identity even against adult pressures. What looks at first glance like a complete abnegation of the specifically-me may in fact be the young person's most effective way of safeguarding the specifically-me until it becomes strong enough to stand alone.

There will be learning going on through all these years, but it may be only a modicum of academic learning, which—since it is largely foreordained by educators for generalized huge populations of students—cannot be suited *cap-à-pie* to the interests and aims of each individual student. Most of the learning of this time, therefore, is likely to be concerned with people and their interrelationships and patterns of interaction, and with searching through various kinds of extracurricular activities to find those that promise to add most to the specifically-me, so that it can ultimately fulfill its aim and goal, which is somehow to imprint itself on its world.

That sounds somewhat grandiose, but it isn't necessarily so. Most of us are content to have some perceptible influence with our own small circle of friends, relatives, and co-workers and to be recognized by them as uniquely ourselves. But how important even that kind of imprint is to us, how vitally important, you discover whenever one of those people forgets your birthday, or credits something that you did to someone else, or neglects to ask your opinion on a matter about which you have some small expertise. And so we work vigorously in our early adulthood, steadily through our middle years, and still persistently in our later years, always trying to become more and more clearly and specifically ourselves.

We can make our personal imprints in a number of ways: by changing something, adding something, or subtracting something, by creating or pro-creating, by reshaping or reordering, even by eradicating or destroying. The shape of the imprint is determined by many forces. Hitler made his imprint by exterminating people; Columbus made his by exterminating the limits of the Old World. But it takes no such monstrous or monumental acts to produce our imprint on our world. One's imprint is made, however modestly, just by being honestly, unmistakably, and unwithholdingly one's self. The important point is that, whether it is good, bad, or indifferent, an imprint cannot be made by an image or by any multiplicity of images. It is the work of the real and effective self.

On Becoming a Good Parent to Oneself

We need, finally, to try to determine how all of these various components of the self-system can be integrated into an efficiently functioning unity capable of promoting our self-esteem and of maintaining it in spite of recurrent threats and occasional severe setbacks.

It is tempting to extend the Sullivan nomenclature one step further and call this integrating force the *generically-me*. To do so would lead more easily into suggesting, for the sake of argument and clarification, that boys are confronted much earlier than girls with the need to define and develop the specifically-me, but that they face later than girls, often with more difficulty, and sometimes with complete refusal, the need to move on into the generically-me. Our cultural stereotype of *male* calls for early and strong individualization in boys, literally self-assertiveness. The counterpart stereotype of *female* calls for girls to be gentle and self-effacing. And insofar as boys and girls pattern themselves after these stereotypes, it is patently easier for girls to become motherly than for boys to become fatherly. Fortunately, the healthier people among us are the least liable to let themselves be encased by cultural stereotypes; and those who really succeed in firmly establishing the specifically-me are well able to move on into the generically-me.

The term is a kind of shorthand identification of the integrating force, but the nature of that force is more cogently conveyed by another way of describing its task, which is learning how to become a good parent to oneself. I came by the phrase and the concept from one of E. Van Norman Emery's lectures, which I can't quote verbatim, but the gist of his statement was that the hallmark of maturity is the ability to be a good parent to oneself.

The process of integration begins fairly soon after the first differentiations of the self-system have taken place. With the emergence of the Observer, that reality-oriented character, the child is forced at times to question the validity of the parent-determined images of good-me and bad-me. Parents do make mistakes, they do sometimes misjudge feelings and motivations. On occasions, even the most conscientious and consistent of parents may mirror to the child the image of good-me exactly when the child's Observer is recording the child's malicious intent; and, contrariwise, may at times mirror the image of bad-me exactly when the child's Observer is registering his innocence. These occasions can be very troubling to the child who sees himself oftener and more clearly as bad-me than as good-me; they may indeed precipitate such dire anxiety that the child either rejects his Observer completely or identifies him with bad-me (in which case, one might wonder if all knowledge is thereafter viewed as guilty knowledge, to be avoided as far as possible).

More secure children, however, seem to deal with these parental misjudgments pragmatically, exploiting them when the error is in the child's favor, and protesting indignantly the errors that disadvantage them. They learn very readily to recognize similar pragmatic operations in other children. Jennifer, at not quite four, lodged her protest about her sister, Laurie, not quite six, like this: "When I hurt Laurie and say I didn't mean to, I really *mean* I didn't mean to, but when she hurts me and says she didn't mean to, she doesn't mean that, at all! She really means to hurt me!" And Jennifer is right. Impulsive and given to running forward while looking backward to laugh over her shoulder, she has frequent collisions, and often with Laurie; whereas Laurie, thoughtful and well coordinated, almost never does anything accidentally. Laurie at six was already fully aware that the words, *"I'm sorry, I didn't mean to,"* are social currency of great value. At the same time she is the child who said, "I didn't see me do it, but the Little Me inside me always sees." Jennifer's I-didn't-mean-to gambit is still as honest as it is instinctive, but when someone else can manage to say it before she can, she is surprised into laughter—and you know that her Observer is on the job.

In ways like these, gradually and more or less steadily children learn to search out and delete what is invalid in the primitive images of good-me and bad-me. Taylor's findings suggest that twelve-year-olds may be wonderfully clear about this matter: of the two hundred children in his study, 81 percent said that they were punished by their parents less than they deserved, and 76 percent said that they were rewarded by their parents less than they deserved (32)! While these responses are susceptible of several different interpretations, one plausible interpretation is that these twelve-year-olds are looking with a critical eye at their parent-determined images of good-me and bad-me, and finding them at considerable variance with reality as the children perceive reality. This is not to say that their perceptions are necessarily accurate ones. It must be remembered that the images in the parents' eyes are also the children's perceptions, and may or may not be congruent with the real attitudes of their parents. But as children grow up, if they grow well, they gradually free themselves from those first global images, and become better able to recognize and adapt to changing attitudes in their parents, and to changing motivations and values in themselves.

Necessarily involved in this process is another: the child's early, global identifications with his parents gradually become partial identifications. He continues to emulate the parental traits that are in accord with his developing ego-ideal, and he stops emulating those that seem irrelevant to what he wants to become. But then, as he grows more and more involved with the fascinating business of becoming specifically-me, only one identification remains important to him, and it is a complete identification—with himself. In adolescence he is likely to reject *in toto* even the partial identifications with his parents. Much of the time they are the last people in the world that he wants to be like in any respect. Not that he has anything against them personally, you understand—it is just that they are the older generation; and what young person in his right mind wants to be like the older generation? They had their day. Now it's the younger generation's turn.

We could say, with a fair degree of accuracy, that there are times in the years of his teens when our young man's specifically-me seems the same thing as his ego-ideal, when his behavior seems epitomized in the exasperated queries of Professor Higgins in *My Fair Lady,* "Oh, why can't a woman be like a man?" culminating in "Why can't a woman be like *me?*"* They are beautiful times, those moments when he is really so tremendously pleased and impressed with himself. But then that dastardly little Observer puts in his two bits' worth and splits those two self-images apart —and the glory of self-adulation turns into abysmal despair. It is at such points, I think, that the young person first begins to be somewhat of a parent to himself, trying both to encourage and to discipline himself, to force himself to face the realities of his situation, and at the same time to hold on to some faith in himself.

It is the harder work because now his real parents keep confusing the issues. *He* no longer stereotypes *them,* he sees them as people, and people with some grievous weaknesses; but now when he is struggling to become self-dependable (and this is what we really mean when we use the commoner term, *self-dependent*), they seem blind to his worst faults and completely unshaken by his most ghastly failures. They seem to have no appre-

---

*Copyright © 1956 by Frederick Loewe and Alan Jay Lerner. Used by permission of Chappell & Company, Inc.

ciation whatsoever either of how far short he falls now of what he ought to be or of how far he will some day surpass all their expectations of him. It is really almost touching that two presumably intelligent people could care so much for him, for so little good reason, and could have such blind faith in him when they don't even know what his aspirations are. Even a child could be more astute than they are. And it is stupid to feel touched and grateful to them. He has every right to be as angry as he is, because all this free caring and blind faith that they give him only make it harder for him to demand proof of worth from himself.

He keeps on being angry with them until one day he realizes that his parents are looking at him and talking with him in a new way, not just as a stereotype of "our son," but as a person in his own right, belonging to himself. That doesn't quite change everything all at once, because they lapse back into old habits easily; but gradually, over time, the new quality in the relationship becomes firmly established, and it brings a large dividend in addition. Now every positive quality that he sees in his parents adds new and positive meaning to their caring for him and believing in him. To be esteemed by stupid people, or to be valued merely as progeny, adds nothing at all to one's self-esteem; but to be valued by the same people whom we value—this not only reinforces our self-esteem, but also strengthens the would-be good parent within us, who can take it as evidence that we are at least on the right track. Then we can begin to retrieve some of the partial identifications with our parents that we had earlier discarded, and to try fitting them again into our ego-ideals, where surprisingly often they now seem to belong. Please note, however, that we are speaking of *partial* identifications, because if they are more than partial or less than carefully selective, they can easily amount to capitulation to the pattern of one's natural parents, which means premature closure and in effect the end of growth in the self-system. That can be a natural and probable outcome, an easy way out of trying through all the rest of one's life to become a good parent to oneself, but it involves risks and disadvantages that we will be wise to consider.

To begin with, great variation exists from one person to another in the relative strengths of the drive toward interpersonal affiliations, on the one hand, and the drive toward imprinting the specifically-me upon one's world, on the other hand. To some of us the approval of those whom we value is basis enough for adequate self-esteem. To others of us such approval, however treasured, remains blind faith, not really merited until we have proved our worth. But great variation can also exist in the relative strengths of these two drives from time to time within the same person. The young woman who in her twenties is quite happy to devote herself completely to her family and friends may find, at forty, that she is not very much needed by anyone any longer, and therefore is no longer sure of her own worth, and has to start all over again her search for the specifically-me. Similarly, the aging man who has paid little attention to his family while he concentrated his energies on his work, to prove his worth, may find himself suddenly very tired and more than a little lonely, and wanting increasingly to enjoy the lost companionship of his family and friends.

Both of these hypothetical people have been somewhat less than good parents to themselves, not foreseeing and safeguarding against the contingencies that later threaten their self-esteem. Both stayed too long, too narrowly, and too unremittingly with the task of their first choice, with the result that when that was done, they found themselves stranded. The wiser strategy, the better parenting, would have kept the two different drives in better balance, so that both approval and proof of worth would be available to them at need.

The question is how to achieve this more desirable outcome. If you will bear with my sounding disconnected for a moment, I want to refer to the finding reported by Raush and Sweet, from a study of the behavior of normal boys as compared to the behavior of disturbed and hyperaggressive boys (22). They found that the normal boys were able (and the other boys were not) to anticipate mounting stresses and to deflect trouble by indulging in "a voluntary regression, with ego choice of time and place." To put it more simply, the normal boys goofed off in situations where goofing off was quite permissible.

The principle need not be limited to regressive behavior. It applies equally well to all of those points of choice where we want to exercise voluntary control, keeping in mind that every step in the actualization of the ego-ideal involves the selection of one alternative and the sacrifice of all others. In the eagerness and ardor with which we set out to imprint ourselves upon our world, we are all too likely to overlook the importance of anticipating the stresses that we may come under from the alternatives that we have sacrificed at the points of choice. And in exactly as much as we are unable to anticipate mounting stresses, in just so much are we handicapped in our attempts to deflect trouble.

When good parents emancipate their adult or near-adult child from parental control, it is because they have gone as far as they can go in preparing him for freedom and for the exercise of his own choice. It remains for each of us, if we are to become good parents to ourselves, to emancipate ourselves from any tyrannical control of our strongest drives. The central and unchanging goal of the mature and integrated self is to chart its own course, to choose its own direction, and this is no easy matter. We have no choice about being born, and few of us choose when and how we die; but between birth and death we can attain to a position of choice if we can learn—early or late, but well—that the direction in which we move is not so important as its being our chosen direction. There is an odd twist to this, too: the direction we take, at any point in time, is the inevitable resultant of all the choices that we have earlier made, willingly or unwillingly, and wittingly or unwittingly; but the minute we consciously decide between alternatives, with some awareness of the possible consequences, and full acceptance of the risk, we have attained to a position of choice, no matter how many other forces may be pressing in on us.

It should be obvious that I like Dr. Emery's definition of maturity, since I have gone to such lengths to elaborate upon it, but in the process of elaborating on it I have arrived at my own grass-roots kind of definition, and I give it to you now, for whatever it may be worth.

Maturity is being able honestly to say, "If I had it to do over again, I'd do it the same way, not because I did it the best way, but because I learned to understand why I did it that way, and how it shaped the next steps for me—because, in short, it seemed to me at the time my best choice, and therefore its results, both good and bad, are appropriately *mine,* an integral part of *me.*"

Chapter 4. PROOF OF WORTH

Up to this point we have discussed work in several different contexts. In our conceptual framework we viewed psychosocial growth as the outcome of more or less successful coping with stress. Whether the expenditure of energy is voluntary or involuntary, it still takes work to grow. Then we considered the kinds of work involved in developing interpersonal relationships and the self-system so as to make reliable psychosocial resources of both of them. But up to this point the emphasis has been chiefly on the stresses, the methods of coping, and the resultant growth, rather than on the work that goes into coping and provides the linkage between stress and growth. Here I want to focus on work, itself, as another psychosocial resource.

In case you are wondering if we are again going to trace an optimal life history from a different viewpoint, the answer is No. This particular psychosocial resource is significantly different from the others in the degree to which it is recognized by the world around us. Generally speaking, our society doesn't seem to care very much if our interpersonal relationships are good or poor, or if our self-esteem is sound or shaky; but it has a whole hierarchy of rewards to bestow upon competent, productive, responsible people, and an even larger hierarchy of punishments to inflict upon incompetent, unproductive, irresponsible people. As many inequities as there are in the distribution of these social rewards and punishments, the fact remains that the social consequences of the work we do, and of the way in which we do it, are widespread and telling. They slot us, at once, into a specific social class (privileged nonworker, upper class, middle class, lower class, unemployable); and then, by generating still further consequences (determining our income, our associates, our opportunities for advance-

ment, or our vulnerability to layoffs), they lock us into those slots. Because
of that locking-in effect, many parents are unable to help their children
to anything better than the parents themselves have had.

To rectify that inequity we must look to the schools. Except as the
schools may provide it, there is no sure and commonly available bridge
between the more or less sheltering home and protecting family, and the
unsheltering, unprotecting, implacably demanding wider world of adulthood. No other course is long enough, no other gradient gradual enough, to
support a child's well-being through the twelve to twice-twelve years that it
takes to develop the skills and behaviors necessary for effective adulthood.
Here, then, in our consideration of work as a psychosocial resource, we
shall be talking primarily about our schools, because it is to them that we
have assigned almost the total task of developing this resource in our children.

Let me try to define the resource itself by reviewing briefly the thinking
that led to our calling it, in our office jargon, C-P-R. In my first attempt to
formulate mental health dimensions, back in the early fifties, I used only
the single term *competence* for this dimension; but every day that I spent
in the schools I was confronted with the problem of children who racked up
fine scores on achievement tests, but never completed their desk work or
homework assignments, who were obviously taking in, but not giving out,
who were competent without being productive. Many adults, too, who are
fully competent to do their jobs, are similarly unproductive, at some times or
regularly, out of dissatisfaction with their working conditions or preoccupation with more personal concerns. And so I added the term *productivity,*
with the implication that one can hardly be productive without first being
competent.

Then in one of those unguarded moments when one's mind plays tricks,
I realized that a good many young people in my caseload had proved at
least their biological competence and productivity by becoming parents, but
could hardly be considered parents in any psychological sense, because they
were quite irresponsible toward their children. Admittedly, that is playing
with words, but there is more than play in it. We have to say, of many a
highly skilled and often productive worker, "He's the best there is, when
he feels like working, but you can't count on him. He'll do it if he pleases,
and if he doesn't please, he won't." Obviously, then, the term *responsibility*
had to be added to the other two terms, to yield a rubric broad enough to
cover all that is involved in effective work. Failure to develop either productivity or responsibility leaves this psychosocial resource as incomplete as
failure to develop competence.

But failure to develop one or another of the three components is not the only difficulty that can arise in this resource. There are two other incomplete combinations that can cause embarrassment. One can feel responsible without being either competent or productive; and perhaps every responsible human being has found himself in that position at one time or another, feeling a pressing obligation to do something that he doesn't know how to do. It is impossible for anyone to develop competence in all fields of endeavor; and the more highly specialized one's own field of endeavor is, the longer it takes to develop proficiency in it, and the less time and energy there is left for developing competence in any other field. Need for a competence that we haven't acquired almost invariably leaves us productive of nothing except blunders. Even when we are competent, an emergency demand, if it is acute enough, can make us unproductive for a space of time by throwing us into "stage fright" or "blocking" (my personal term for it, since it afflicts me almost every time I start to write a paper, is "verbal *paralysis agitans*").

This resource, then, consists of three components that may develop at different rates and to widely differing levels. It is also, like the other psychosocial resources, vulnerable to unforeseen or sudden sharp stress, even when all three components have been developed to an appropriate degree. Again we have the best of reasons for seeing to it that we have more than just one resource, so that when one fails us, another can be called into auxiliary service.

The immediate question that arises when we start to consider work as a psychosocial resource is simply, How can you reasonably call it that? How can you get rid of all the negatives attached to going to school or to work? Who likes to hear the alarm clock sounding off? Who doesn't watch the clock more and more often as quitting time draws near? Who doesn't grouch about the irksomeness of work—about having to keep regular hours, or about not being allowed to keep regular hours, about having no variety in our tasks, or about not being able to predict from day to day what tasks will be assigned to us; about always having too much to do, or about never having enough to keep us busy; about being supervised to within an inch of our lives, or about being held accountable for getting a job done, without being given any advice about how to do it?

The prevalence of all of these negatives has to be acknowledged; but we can oppose to them one highly provocative and potent fact: that in the beginning, work is play. That is an overbroad statement that requires immediate modification. A baby crying out of hunger or pain or sleepiness is working, not playing; he is reacting to the stress of unmet primary needs.

But—as Robert White puts it—"when its primary needs are satisfied and its homeostatic chores are done, an organism is alive, active, and up to something" (34). The rested, happy, well-fed baby is an explorer, investigating with lively curiosity his hands, his feet, his mother's face, his toys —anything and everything within his purview. This is play, but it is also learning and doing; in essence precisely the same kind of activity that ultimately adds up to our acquiring education and developing valuable work-skills.

This kind of work, beginning in play and after the primary needs have been met, is the kind that can become a psychosocial resource. But we still call it work, instead of play, and I think this is because we continue to distinguish between work and play as school children do: "play" is any activity that you engage in when you want to and because you want to; and "work" is any activity that you engage in when you don't want to, but because someone else demands it. The difference lies not in the activity involved, which may be precisely the same activity, but in whether we engage in it by choice or under coercion.

This may not say much for our rationality, but it reflects clearly how we prize our autonomy—at least, whenever we are feeling strong and able to cope. The trouble is that society insists upon trying to socialize us, which means that it requires us to surrender some part of our autonomy. It is beside the point that to claim autonomy without having the necessary skills to back it up is risky business (as every child knows who has spurned the helping hand when he first tries to ice-skate). The point is only that to have to do what someone else tells you to do is enough to make the activity, whatever it is, just plain unpleasant. Until we recognize that little fact, and find effective ways to counterbalance the unpleasantness, we are not likely to change our largely negative attitudes toward work.

But to get off dead center we need only shift the subject half an inch —from *work* to *our work,* one's own work, whatever it may be. Our own work is by way of being the marriage contract that each of us makes with the society that we live in. It may not always be a psychosocial resource, because here, too, there are good marriages and bad ones; but it becomes a resource just as soon and as far as it attests visibly to our proof of worth. By virtue of demonstrating our competence, it supports and nourishes our self-esteem. By virtue of demonstrating our responsibility, it strengthens and enriches our relationships with our significant Others. And by virtue of demonstrating that by our own activity we can change something in the world around us, it restores to us again (and not greatly changed from what it was in early childhood) that joy in doing that is the wellspring of productivity.

All that we have to do now is to determine how we can best help children, during and via their school years, to develop the skills and the interests that may enable them to choose the work they do thereafter, work that each then can think of possessively as "my work." I am taking for granted your understanding that while we are doing this, we shall also be trying to determine how to increase the competence, the productivity, and the responsibility of all of us who work in schools.

Competence

Whenever the subject of competence is broached, the question of IQ is sure to follow. We may as well, therefore, try to deal with that question at once. I want to exclude from this discussion the Mongoloids, the cretins, the demonstrably brain-damaged; they are special cases whose special needs have been recognized and are now, at least in some small part, beginning to be met.

For the sake of gaining a fresher outlook on the question of IQ, as it applies to the rest of the population, let me advance an absurd proposition and then, by saying in what ways it is absurd, perhaps begin to clear up some common misunderstandings. The proposition might be put as follows: If we could adequately test newborn infants for what we loosely call "intelligence," we should not find them distributed in our hallowed bell-shaped curve, on a base of well over a hundred points. We should be more likely to find them clustered in a rectangular distribution on a base of perhaps no more than twenty points.

The first absurdity in this proposition is that no self-respecting test-constructor would consider a test "adequate" unless it yielded a bell-shaped distribution. As Garrett puts it, test-makers set about their task with "the normal hypothesis" definitely in mind, so that the resulting bell-shaped curve is evidence of the success of their efforts "rather than . . . conclusive proof of the 'normality' of the trait being measured" (6). Or as Edwards, another statistician, puts it, "our observations have been forced into discrete categories by the nature of the testing instrument" (4). The second absurdity is that what we usually mean by the term *intelligence* is almost completely potential in newborn infants, still awaiting development and therefore not yet measurable. This is not to say that newborns do not vary widely in many respects—quite the contrary. As scientists find more and more ways to detect fine differences in more and more structures and functions of the human organism (or for that matter, in any animal), it becomes increasingly clear that the "normal" range of variation between individuals is very wide, indeed (5). It is certainly possible that some of these even-now-measurable differences are significantly related to the IQ potential of the newborn. But we shall still be stuck with the fact that how and to what degree that potential becomes actualized is determined by its interaction with its environment, perhaps most crucially during the first year of life (11).

The interaction between potential and environment is built into all of our most widely used IQ tests. They are standardized on child populations that have been exposed to such interaction long enough for the differences in actualized IQ to be measurable. Thus, we find a wide range of IQ scores in school children, but their scores are not so much a reflection of their native endowment as they are reflections of how their native endowment has been shaped by their life experiences and their interactions with the world around them, and of how much of that shaping the particular IQ test taps (9, 12).

We can continue the argument now by formulating another proposition, again not easily testable, but not—I think—absurd. If we could somehow, by some magic, eliminate from our behavior all effects due to hostility, to panic, to guilt or anxiety or other disruptive emotions, there would be very little left to deserve the term *stupidity*. Many of us, looking back on our most embarrassing blunders, or our most wasteful and destructive mistakes, realize that *we were not surprised* at the outcome, which means, it seems to me, that these blunders were not due to our incapacity to understand cause-and-effect relationships, but were rather the result of some unbridled impulse overriding our regard for cause and effect.

Unfortunately, the matter cannot be dismissed there, on a light note. There is an underlying and gravely concerning implication to be noted. If disruptive feelings occur soon enough and often enough in a child's life, they can effectively block him in cognitive learning, the most important part of which is understanding cause-and-effect relationships. When children cannot recognize the negative quality of their feelings, they cannot see any connection between those feelings and the reactions they provoke in others. Because they see themselves as behaving innocently, they are astonished and hurt and angry when they find themselves "misunderstood." Recognizing our ulterior motives permits us to learn from experience; not recognizing them precludes such learning. In either case we look stupid at the time, defeated in our conscious aims by our unconscious intent.

There is such a wealth of empirical data putting the IQ in its proper place that it is difficult to summarize briefly, but let us begin with data dealing with the instability of IQ scores in children. We do not yet have any intelligence tests that permit us to predict from an infant's score what that same child's score will be when he starts to school, let alone what it will be in adulthood. It is often argued that the use of different tests at different age-levels is enough to account for the lack of correlation; but later on, beginning in the school years, the use of different tests at different age-levels may yield fairly high correlations. In general, IQ scores tend to increase after children enter school, but they may also decrease (25, 31), and year-to-year fluctuations are common. *After* four or five years of schooling, children's IQ scores tend to become more stable, but before then they are rather more sensitive indicators of how children are reacting to their environment than of how much "intelligence" they have. Perhaps the clincher in this line of evidence is the finding of the Fels Research Institute investigators that the best single predictor of success in adulthood is the amount of *IQ gain* from age six to age ten (25).

Such evidence points to early experience as a factor strongly affecting the IQ, and again there are multiple studies to confirm that idea. Experimentalists working with animals, particularly rabbits and chimpanzees, have found that when animals, normal at birth, are reared from birth in total darkness, they become blind. In the absence of light stimulation the ganglion cells of the retina and the optic nerve fibers atrophy, and the process at length becomes irreversible (18,19). A similar kind of process occurs in the psychosocial development of human infants. From the day of birth they need mothering and social stimulation in amounts well beyond those required just to meet their physical needs, and if they are significantly deprived of that essential early social stimulation, they can be permanently damaged in learning capacity (17, 26, 27, 28). One of the most appalling things in our society today is that we are permitting untold numbers of children to be so damaged when we could prevent it. We have tried with our Head Start programs, and with innovative projects of greater depth (1), to reduce the incidence of learning failures in underprivileged children by offering them enriched environments in what used to be their preschool years, but these will never achieve maximal effectiveness until there is wider, more general understanding of the continuing influence of stimulation on intelligence. As Riesen puts it, "We may tentatively conclude that brain cells, like muscle cells, are dependent upon exercise" (20).

There are, of course, positive as well as negative effects of early experience. For example, there has been a significant upward shift in the norms, over those earlier established, on the Gesell, the Cattell, and the Viennese infant developmental scales (10). Babies now sit alone, stand alone, and learn to walk at appreciably earlier ages than before. Since we have not been "breeding for intelligence," it is hypothesized that this earlier learning, as well as the accompanying increase in body size, is due in part to better nutrition and medical supervision, and in part to the change in our ways of dressing babies. Free of swaddling clothes, they can move more easily, and their increased mobility stimulates their motor development.

Both the positive and the negative effects of early experience are vividly documented by the Skeels and Skodak studies of orphanage children (23, 24). Their subjects were twenty-five children considered, for various reasons, to be unsuitable for placement in adoptive homes. Twelve of them, tested at an average age of seventeen months, and having an average IQ of 87, remained in the orphanage. The other thirteen, tested at an average age of eighteen months, and averaging 64 in IQ, were placed in a home for mentally retarded girls and women, where they were lavishly loved and cared for by the older inmates. Twenty months later, those thirteen children were again tested and were found to have gained an average of 27.5 points in IQ, making them eligible for placement in adoptive homes.

By contrast, the children who remained in the cold, sterile, unstimulating environment of the orphanage were found, when they were tested thirty months later, to have lost in IQ score by an average 26.2 points. In less than three years the initial 23-point difference in average IQ between these two groups of children had been reversed and increased to a 32-point difference in favor of the children who had the benefit of a close and loving one-to-one relationship with their caretakers, who—perhaps *because* of being feebleminded—were better able to communicate with two- and three-year-olds than are many highly intellectualized adults.

More recent studies are pinpointing the importance of interpersonal communication for the ways in which small children learn or fail to learn in their first few years of life, and a more basic approach than our Head Start programs is focused on teaching mothers how to communicate better with their babies (8). Where that communication is full and clear and simple, and skillfully paces the baby's comprehension, the baby's understanding grows apace. Where the communication is restricted, ambiguous, or either far beyond the baby's grasp or too readily within it, his growth in understanding is slow and stultified.

But this is not yet the whole story. A third line of evidence points to the operation of other factors than the IQ as among the primary determinants of learning or of failure to learn in childhood years. Anxiety (22), hyperactivity (33), discouragement and other kinds of emotional disturbance (15, 28) often outweigh IQ in their effects on cognitive learning. In our St. Louis county studies of academic progress patterns we had two samples of underachieving children, amounting to almost 200 cases, and in both samples we found a bell-shaped distribution of IQ: almost 15 percent had IQ's ranging from 80 to 89, slightly over 70 percent had IQ's ranging from 90 to 110, and about 15 percent had IQ's over 110 (32, 33). Obviously, poor achievement cannot be attributed just to poor intelligence, although there are disturbing indications that continued poor achievement may contribute significantly to reducing IQ scores (31).

On the other hand, Rosenthal and Jacobson have reported finding that when teachers were told that certain children had exceptional promise, those children outperformed their classmates of equivalent intelligence (21). While that finding is not going unchallenged (good teachers being far more astute about children's potentials and motivations than the finding seems to imply), there is general agreement that the majority of children, like most of the rest of us, try to live up to what is expected of them. But notice the seldom-formulated corollary of that statement: every time this involves living down to others' expectations, we waste human potential. And we waste it, extravagantly, by programing children through school, in the lower grades on the basis of their IQ scores primarily, in the upper grades on the basis of their measured aptitudes.

We are by no means so simple or so obvious as our IQ scores or our measurable aptitudes. All of us are reservoirs of undeveloped (and therefore unmeasured and often unguessed) potentials that, given motivation and opportunity, we could develop. Look at the productions of the Association of Handicapped Artists, paintings done with the brush held between the teeth or between the toes, and the poorest of them far superior in technical skill to what most of us could produce with good right hands. Or consider the fact that during the Renaissance all cultivated individuals were expected to be able to compose and play music and to write verse, simply as social graces, like dancing; and the result was a wealth of music and poetry, much of it short of greatness, but good out of all proportion to the amount of talent and "giftedness" that would be expected today from a comparable population. *We limit what children could learn to do,* because we have tests that show very *wide differences between them in what they have already learned to do* by the time they enter school.

I am going to propose that the attainment of competence depends primarily on just three things—opportunity, motivation, and discipline. There is overlap among these three, but if we discuss them in that order we may be able to minimize repetition.

For children, opportunity is given or withheld first by their parents, and then by the teachers who are stationed at regular intervals all along the way of the bridge that is school, and by others of us (like mental health personnel) who may be involved with children from time to time. Unfortunately, we tend to be so concerned to give children the opportunities that we have decided they ought to have, that we deny them many opportunities that they want. We rationalize this beautifully by saying that it is better for children to succeed than to fail, and there is more than a modicum of truth in that; but it encourages us to leave a lot of potential undeveloped. Motivated children are not so much hurt by failing as by being *stuck with failure,* by being denied the opportunity to change initial failure into eventual success. And this is precisely what we do to them when we program them through school on the basis of their measured aptitudes.

The fact is that if they want enough to learn, children with no aptitude for art can learn to paint and model, children with no aptitude for sports can learn to become fairly proficient in sports, and children with no aptitude for singing can learn to sing: and their self-concepts are enlarged and strengthened by such learning, and their lives enriched. I say this with the more conviction because I have had periodic misgivings about it, most recently when my two little grandnieces clamored to learn some of the songs from *Fiddler on the Roof,* and I set out to teach them. They are not likely to become singing stars, but where at first they seemed to be completely tone-deaf, they can now produce recognizable melodies; and they may, like their mother who started in the same way, make the Glee Club in college if their motivation continues.

If we define opportunity simply as freedom of action and freedom of access, then it becomes at once quite clear that only if we do not plan, organize, and direct children's activities through every minute of their waking hours are they free to explore and to search out the new things that can engage their interest. Only if we allow them access to what is in the world around them, including us, will their lively curiosity be free to learn about the world around them. If we really want to enlarge their opportunities, we must learn better how to entertain them—and I mean "entertain" not only in the usual active sense of interesting, amusing, and stimulating them, but also, and more importantly, in the quieter sense of inviting them, welcoming them, and offering them as much as we have to offer.

To avoid misunderstanding I am going to anticipate here and add a comment about discipline. Whenever we entertain, in the way just described, we are being host or hostess, and by virtue of that fact we have a right to expect our guests to abide by the customs of the house, whether "the house" is the home or the classroom or an office. Some children will be slow to grasp what is expected of them as "guests"; others may be unwilling or unable at first to conform to "the customs of the house." The requirements should be explained as simply and lucidly as possible, but a child's continuing failure to heed them calls—not for a pitched battle between child and teacher in the presence of other children, but for the child's temporary removal from the room. I realize that this practice has fallen into disrepute with many good educators, but I think that is due to our not taking enough care to make the exclusion a learning experience for the child. The exclusion should never be for a stipulated length of time, but only for so long as it takes the child to decide that he would rather conform to the rule than sit alone outside the classroom door. Most children will make the decision in a matter of minutes.

To see how opportunity and discipline combine with motivation to increase competence, let us recall briefly the healthy hypothetical child of our earlier discussions. His first turning over in his crib would perhaps have been more accident than anything else, but after a few weeks he is twisting and turning and squirming, struggling to roll himself over, and when he finally manages it, he beams with delight. He works as hard, shows the same astonishing persistence, at learning to sit alone, to crawl, then to stand alone, and eventually to take his first steps alone. His motivation is strong and urgent, and his joy in each new accomplishment is unmistakable. But this lucky child has parents who not only give him ample opportunity, but also show him instantly and unmistakably that they, too, delight in his every advance toward increasing competence. Thus he experiences very early the first social rewards for his successful efforts: his parents are pleased with him and proud of him.

By the time, then, when he has to begin to learn the not-fun kinds of learning, he is already quite clear about the fact that his learning will bring his parents' approval, and his not learning will bring their disapproval. He will not always choose to do what his parents want him to do. He will have to test from time to time to see if they really meant what they said, or if they might have forgotten that they said it. But he will have gone along with them often enough (a) to have learned to do what they asked him to learn to do, (b) to feel pride in his gradually increasing competence, and (c) to have acquired considerable confidence in his ability to learn.

And so at the time of his school entry he will have at least an age-appropriate degree of competence. He will be able to dress and undress himself, to take care of his toileting alone, to wash himself (not to any look of scrubbed cleanliness, but well enough to show that he has had some transaction with soap and water), and he will be able to express himself verbally and to understand what others say to him. He will be hyperalerted for a few days, because for a small child to start to school is a very big step into the unknown; but he will enter with real eagerness, in spite of his trepidation. He will still be strongly motivated to increase his competence day by day and week by week. In short, he will be a self-starter, ready to go.

But not all children are self-starters when they enter school. There is great diversity among those others; about all that they seem to have in common, besides being children, is the inadequacy of their coping strengths. As we tentatively conceptualize (33) what happens to these children early in their school careers (the exact time depending largely on the kind of teacher that they have), they seem first to fall into two groups. Some of them, having been overexposed to stress too great for them to handle successfully, are apprehensive from the start. Others, having been underexposed to stress, are self-assured to begin with; but as soon as school stresses impinge upon them, they become upset. Both groups can be distinguished from the self-starters by their manifest conviction that school work is very hard work. This was wonderfully demonstrated to us a few years ago, when we were taking primary children one at a time from the classroom, to put them through a series of simple tasks. The instructions for one task were: "Now with your left hand touch your right ear." The self-starters smiled, thought for an instant, and then put hand to ear. The others looked worried, took a few seconds longer to think the problem through, and then each in his own turn arrived at the same solution and made the valiant effort, wrapping his left arm around behind his head to reach his right ear!

In the children who start school with inadequate coping strengths and therefore find or make all school work difficult, the motivation to learn is quickly reduced to the motivation to please—to please teacher or parents or both. If they can please their important Others without learning to be more competent, they will happily let the matter rest at that. If, however, they must increase their competence in order to please their important Others, then they quickly divide again, into three groups, on the basis of the strength of their motivation to please. One group we call "the strugglers." They are children who will work assiduously, even inveterately, to become more competent, not because in itself that gives them any joy, but because it brings them approval. The second group we call "the nonstrugglers"; they have either too little energy, or too little hope of pleasing, to make any sustained attempt to become competent. The third group we call "the rebels," and impute to them a refusal to bargain on these terms—essentially, a bitter intrinsic motivation *not* to learn, if that is to be the only basis on which others will value them.

To ask any teacher to deal differentially with all of these different kinds of children is to ask a great deal. By way of suggesting a simpler solution, let me cite three classroom situations. Twelve years ago I watched a gifted first-grade teacher tease her students into learning, giving them an assignment, shaking her head over its difficulty and murmuring that it really was too hard for first-graders and she didn't think that they could do it, but adding that if they fooled her, if they really could do it, then she would give them a few more like it the next day. Every child in the class completed the assignment, and whooped with enthusiasm at the prospect of having more work to do the next day. There was no trickery in what Faye Anastasoff did. The children were as well aware as she was that she was playing a game with them—but they liked the game.

Five years ago I watched Dr. Robert Davis film a class session with fourth-graders from one of the poorest slum areas in St. Louis, where for years there had been almost no motivation to learn anything academic, let alone "the new math." And yet the most striking thing about the session was the eager, often excited interest of the children in the class work. As I tried to analyze how he was generating such eagerness, I realized that, far from putting himself between the children and their tasks so that he might better help them with the work, he was deliberately keeping himself well out of the way, as if he could thus create a vacuum in which the children and what they were trying to learn would be drawn together. He describes this as leaving the children free to "discover" how the new math works, and considers the children's response to be their natural lively interest in exploration, and their elation over eventual discovery (2).

Two years ago I heard William R. Page describe his work with academically retarded seventh-graders in a project designed to offer them "a comprehensive remedial and developmental program."* One of the key objectives of the program was to convey to the students that they themselves were responsible for their learning, the teacher serving only as a resource person to them if they wanted help. When the students entered the special classroom, they were told frankly that they were there because of their academic retardation, and that they would have there an opportunity to learn whatever they wanted to learn; no one would try to force them to work—if they chose not to work, they might play quiet games or just sit, but they would not be permitted to keep anyone else from working. These statements were repeated as often as necessary to make the message clear,

---

*Speech at Mental Health Grand Rounds, St. Louis County Health Dept., Clayton, Mo., January 17, 1969.

and it was soon found that almost all of the students were working and enjoying it, were relating more happily to each other and to their teachers, and were learning. Most of them made more than a year's academic progress in less than a year's time.

Explicitly or implicitly the teachers were making statements to the students in all three of those classroom situations. In the first case the statement was a tongue-in-cheek "I bet you can't!" In the second case it was a simple "Do you want to?" In the third case it was an unequivocally clear "It's up to you. We're here to help you only if you want help." All three statement contain a twofold message: first, that to work is a privilege; and second, that each child is free to choose whether or not he wants that privilege.

The markedly accelerated learning that occurred in all three classroom situations suggests that something in the double message stimulated the intrinsic motivation to learn. All children are intrinsically motivated to do *something:* self-starters to learn, strugglers to please, nonstrugglers to retreat from stress, and rebels to refuse to learn. Moreover, all children choose to learn or not to learn, whether we "allow" them to choose or not. There is no way of compelling them to learn anything except the cold hard fact that some people are more powerful than others—specifically, that parents and principals and teachers are more powerful than children and therefore can punish them at will. But punishment cannot elicit intrinsic motivation to learn, and the question is, What can? In these three classroom situations, What did?

The answer, I would speculate, lies in the interpersonal process generated by the teachers' statements. First the children received quite clearly the message that the teachers recognized the choice as the children's to make, and they found this recognition highly gratifying and related more positively to the teachers because of it. Being accorded the freedom to choose released in some of them the natural desire to learn, and in all of them an almost involuntary *quid pro quo,* a willingness to work for teachers who themselves considered it a privilege to work, but still respected children's rights. And finally, and still relating to their positive response to such teachers, they quickly sensed what the outcome would be if they chose not to work, and rejected that outcome. In none of the situations was the alternative made explicit; but it was implicit in all of them that the students who chose not to learn would be out of step and liable to being ignored by their teachers and rejected by their classmates.

Here discipline enters the picture, and I want to digress long enough to make a distinction between punishment and discipline. I use the term *punishment* to mean those personal retaliatory acts that we commit in order to "get even" for a felt personal injury or affront. We can then reserve the term *discipline* to cover only the consequences—spelled out in advance, as "the rules of the game"—that result from certain specified causal behaviors. Punishment entraps learning in the snarl of interpersonal conflicts. Discipline, in the sense in which I am using the term here (which incidentally is its etymological sense), can be carried out by the adult and accepted by the children with complete and mutual good will, although it works to better advantage in a generally warm and entertaining milieu than in a cold and inflexible one. Its function in the development of competence is to give children direct experience in cause-and-effect relationships, thus providing them with accurate feedback by means of which they can learn how to direct their own activities in order to achieve specific desired results. Over time it strengthens children not only by promoting their learning, but also by enhancing their autonomy at each step along the way.

There is no teaching technique more effective than good discipline, and there is almost certainly none that is more difficult to master. Optimally it begins with the teacher clarifying the choices open to the children—whether to learn or not to learn, to learn now or later, or well or poorly, to conform to the rules for classroom behavior or not to conform. But before the children make their choices, the teacher must also clarify for them the outcome that will attach to each of the possible courses of action they might take, and these must all be reasonable and logical outcomes. This calls for thoughtful analysis and planning, both in the interest of fairness and (as a word of warning) with an eye to the teacher's own capacity to adhere to the rules of the game as she formulates them. Unless she keeps the rules few enough and simple enough so that she herself can handle them with ease and complete consistency, she will quickly find herself in trouble and the children out of hand, and with punishment rather than discipline the order of the day.

Finally, once the rules of the game have been established and made clear, the teacher must scrupulously refrain from intervening to spare the children the consequences of their choices, even when the consequences are, for the time being, hurtful to them. To protect a child from the consequences of his own choice, when he has been told what those consequences would be, is not only no kindness to him, but is actively misleading and confusing him, preventing him from getting any grasp of cause-and-effect relationships.

One other aspect of discipline deserves consideration. The fun part of learning lies in discovery, whether it comes through sudden insight or through repetitions of trial and error. But the fun part of learning does not by itself constitute competence. It is only the beginning of it. If competence is to grow and enlarge, then increasingly greater amounts of the work have to be relegated to habit, and this involves considerable quantities of repetitive practice. Only when the alphabet and the multiplication tables and other such implements of academic competence have become familiar enough to have seeped down into the unconscious does the conscious mind become free to work and play on the growing edge of competence. We tend to be so impressed with children who learn by quick insight that we excuse them from practice, with two deleterious effects: these bright children are left with some degree of deficiency in basic skills, and there is put upon them the total task of finding out through (sometimes harsh) experience what they could have learned by precept—for example, that a stitch in time may save nine.

In fact, of course, even the youngest of school children are capable of understanding, if it is explained to them, that practice is necessary for the mastery of basic educational skills. They already know, in connection with fun, that it takes practice to acquire skill and mastery in climbing trees and jungle gyms, in skating, bicycling, jumping rope, or in any other activity that is difficult when first attempted, but becomes fun when mastered. Practice need not be as drearily boring as it is in the average classroom. Since time began, wise teachers have found ways of sweetening practice by putting it into games or music. We have *The Alphabet Song*, we have any number of counting-out rhymes and counting-out songs. With brisk band music, a little free space, and a teacher willing to play drum major, thirty-two children at a time can learn left and right and multiplication, addition, subtraction, and division by a marching drill that they will be ready and eager to repeat as often as they are permitted. There is nothing to keep us from developing similar techniques for all practice needs, unless we are just too lazy, or harbor some leftover childish belief that it is improper to have fun in a classroom.

The argument usually advanced against rote learning is that it is important for children to learn to understand subject content; but what is there really for primary children to understand about why five does not equal six, except that their senses tell them that it doesn't, or about why the sky is blue but the wind blew hard, except that two words that sound alike have different meanings if spelled differently? There is a place for rote learning in the early grades, and children take to it naturally and do it happily if they do it in chorus, with a snap and a crackle. The faster-learning children tend to set the pace, but they still have in their early school years enough of a one-for-all-and-all-for-one feeling that they seem intuitively to set the pace where most of the slower-learning children can be swept along by the tempo. Here and there you will find a child who can help by devising games to sweeten practice. Laurie, starting third grade, has found a new word-game that she is elaborating with great glee. Over a weekend she produced four versions, each distinct from the other except in the ending, which she insists must always be the same. The fourth version goes like this:

A answers B, B bugs C, C counsels D,
D dims E, E echoes F, F finds G,
G gets H, H hides I, I injures J,
J jiggles K, K kicks L, L licks M,
M minds N, N names O, O opens P,
ᴘ pinches Q, Q quiets R, R remembers S,
S suggests T, T tricks U, U unwinds V,
V ventures W, W washes X, X excites Y,
Y yowls "Z!", Z zooms————————"GOOD-BY!"

It remains now only to point out, and to urge that teachers point out, the relationship of competence to self-esteem. There is intrinsic satisfaction in becoming competent in any kind of skill, because it constitutes evidence that an engagement with stress has had a successful outcome. This strengthens one's self-esteem. It is additionally and especially gratifying when others recognize our competence and give us credit for it. This strengthens our motivation to become increasingly competent. And while it is obvious, I think, that I consider it malpractice to give E for effort, without regard to actual competence, we nevertheless shortchange ourselves if we overlook or underestimate the importance of the effort that goes into the attainment of competence. The most significant increment to self-esteem lies not so much in being competent as in knowing that we became so by our own effort, not so much in receiving credit as in knowing that we earned it.

Productivity

A competence once acquired can be maintained at minimal expense in upkeep. Skills solidly based on practice, until they are built into habit, become what we commonly call "second nature," so that even after fairly long periods of disuse they come back quickly and easily when needed. Because they are know-how, they have a rare kind of permanency: the more they are used, the better they become.

This is not true, in the same way, of productivity. Where competence is the result of acquiring skills (incorporating something into ourselves that was not there before), productivity is quite literally expressing a part of ourselves into the world outside, so that it becomes clearly perceptible to others—something that others can see or hear or touch or taste or experience, as when we paint a picture, give a lecture, build a seesaw, bake a pie, or comfort and protect a frightened child. In doing any of these things we extrude a part of ourselves, our energies and our skills, into the world outside of us, and this is a one-way process: the actualization of potential cannot be reversed and the potential reincorporated in us as the same potential that it was before.

To produce, then, is going to deplete us unless (a) we produce only out of our surplus energy, out of supplies over and above those required for day-by-day coping and growing, or (b) what we produce brings us other rewards capable somehow of replenishing our energies. The small child who pats and rolls mud into the shape of cookies or marbles or snakes, or piles leaves or grass clippings to make a snug nest to sit in, is producing out of surplus energy, and he will keep on producing in this way, with evident joy, until his surplus of energy is gone, whereupon his play is suddenly no longer fun, and he quits it forthwith.

That same child, in school a few years later, can't just quit and go home when he runs out of surplus energy. Instead, he has to dig into his reserves in order to keep on producing, and he grows irritable and clumsy. He breaks the point of his pencil, and when he starts toward the pencil sharpener, he knocks his book off his desk, and when he tries to pick up his book, he crumples or tears the paper he was working on. Two minutes after the last bell rings, he is out on the playgound and racing around, apparently as full of energy as he had been in the early morning. He is producing nothing, however, except heat and noise and a little chaos. What looks like surplus energy is in fact not at all available for more productivity, because it has to go into the service of his homeostatic chores. Being harnessed to work through most of the school day has built up tensions in him, and he has to discharge these and feel free and comfortable again, and then go on to eat and sleep before his energies can once more reach a surplus level.

Few of us, as adults, are free to do what the very small child does when his interest in his work-play wanes. We can't just quit. Many of us, however, are like the school boy, being more or less adequately productive in our work but not exactly enamored of it and therefore depleted by producing, so that we have to use the intervals between work periods for reestablishing our homeostatic balance. We may feel some intrinsic satisfaction in being productive, but if we feel inadequately compensated, either in cash or in credit, for being productive, we are not likely to be able to build up a surplus of energy through our work. We have to look elsewhere for the rewards that can replenish us.

What is amiss with most of us in this respect is that without being in love with our work, we are nevertheless wedded to it. I have a gruesome, outrageously humorous recollection that is pertinent here. On the day when the first A-bomb was dropped on Hiroshima, three of us sat listening to the radio in the cyclotron office. For months the cyclotron had been producing only isotopes for medical purposes, but earlier we had been part of a much larger crew, and we had known what we were doing when the cyclotron was producing plutonium. As we listened to the broadcast, our young chief physicist groaned and—head in hand—said: "I know now how the woman felt when they wheeled her into the delivery room, and she started yelling, 'I've changed my mind—I don't want a baby! I've changed my mind!' "

What concerned us then, and what we always have to reckon with, is the fact that a product (in that case, isotopes of one kind or another) may be good or bad, depending upon the uses to which it is put, and once you have produced something, you have no way of ensuring that it will be put to good uses only. But it is the other point of the story that is more immediately relevant to this discussion. For most of us there comes a time when it is too late to change our minds about what kind of work we want to do. We should therefore ensure as far as we can that we choose well in the first place, and this means that the school years should lay the groundwork that will enable us to choose well. Failure to lay the groundwork then results in that terribly common disorder that I call "the end-of-school syndrome." It takes different forms at different ages and in different communities, but it is epidemic in many schools. For the poor students who become dropouts at the earliest legal opportunity, it is marked primarily by depression. In secondary schools where it is common for new graduates to go to work rather than to go on to college, it looks more manic-depressive, with a slight edge of panic. At the college level in the senior year it is somewhat better contained, except for the almost desperate eagerness to have as much fun as possible while it is still possible. At the graduate level it is marked by sudden unexplainable failures in just one subject, or by a devastating onset of abulia, a complete loss of willpower to complete a thesis or dissertation. At whatever level it occurs, it is still comparable to a pre-wedding panic, set off by recognizing that one is on the way to a point from which there is no turning back.

But just as there is nothing quite so efficacious in conquering the pre-wedding panic as consciously knowing that one really does want to get married and to one particular person, so there is nothing more efficacious in allaying the "end-of-school syndrome" than consciously knowing that one wants to go to work, and that this particular kind of work is what one wants to do.

Only in our school years can we safely and economically shop around among possible careers, *if the school permits.* Too many schools do not permit that kind of shopping. They tend, rather, to restrict children's choices and to force premature closure on them by educational counseling and track systems that reflect primarily, and sometimes exclusively, only what the adults in charge deem most appropriate for the children. I am not questioning the good intentions of most "adults in charge," and of course they know more than the children know; but we can know a great deal more than the children know and still not know the children. Until we have research that documents the value *to children* of the judgments that we make for them, we had better keep questioning our logic and our motives, and keep watching to see what happens to the children in the long run.

We say, for example, that we must shape the task to the slow-learning student so as to maximize his opportunity to taste success. Not quite in the same breath, but often very nearly so, we say that the faster-learning students need the stimulation of stiff competition—which means that we minimize their chances to taste success. We take the responsibility for charting their courses for them, on the assumption that we can do this more judiciously than they could (we know so much?), and we largely disregard the well-documented fact that people learn best what they want to learn. If you listen to the children, as children or as adults, what you hear is hardly reassuring.

The feelings of those put early into the slow tracks are somewhat overstated, but not by much, in a bitter little piece called "Soliloquy of a Dropout," the gist of which is: "Against all human dignity, THEY clothed me with condescension, THEY fed me with ashes," peaking to a plea for one last favor, namely, that *they* break the mold that *they* made for *him* (13).

Those in the middle tracks feel consigned to mediocrity, that being the connotation almost invariably attached to being "average." They could suffer worse fates; but how many aspirations and potentialities are nipped in the bud by repeated assurances that there is nothing about being average that one has to be ashamed of?

The children in the fast tracks are more conflicted, because they are the chosen; but they are also the driven. Whatever gain may accrue to their self-esteem from being the chosen is more than offset by the damage they sustain through being driven by adult pressures along courses that adults choose for them. Haggard, studying forty-five high achievers over a five-year period, found that by seventh grade they had accepted adult norms and expectations, but had become increasingly rejecting of adults as persons, showed increased anxiety, aggressiveness, and competitiveness, and decreased originality and creativity. They were leaders in their age groups, but more respected than liked. Few of them were happy children (7). How distressed they may be was brought home to me forcefully when a mother told me that she had given her teen-aged daughter a paper I wrote, years ago, on the dangers of accelerated learning programs (29). The girl had burst into tears, reading it, and asked, "Why can't they see it? Why do they have to push us so?"

The pertinent question is not, to paraphrase Eble (3), whether children can master prescribed curriculum content faster, but whether they might not be better employed in trying their hands and minds at many kinds of activities, in gaining as much exposure as possible to the different kinds of work being done in the world, so that later, when it is time for them to decide upon a career, they will already have had a sampling of many careers. If no better means is available, one easy means is almost always at hand: let each class have a parents' and grandparents' day once a year, inviting them to tell the class what kind of work each does, what its satisfactions are, and what its disadvantages.

But somehow, and quickly, we must learn how to provide in our schools opportunities for children to have many different kinds of learning experiences, work experiences, and play experiences. We must become accepting, if not actively encouraging, of their tendency to shift interest from this activity to that and then to another, instead of requiring them to declare their vocational intentions as they enter high school or even junior high. Few people in this country would advocate arranging marriage contracts for children. Few would consider it wise, as a rule, for couples to marry who have dated only each other, never anyone else. And yet we have become almost as extreme as the British in our haste to slot children into academic tracks out of which, if they can move at all, they can usually only move downward.

If we are to give them reasonable opportunity in their school years to sample many different fields of endeavor, we shall have to open all classes to all applicants, with only some such simple stipulation as that failure to do adequate work in the first quarter will constitute the basis for their exclusion from that class for the rest of the year. The educational counselor would be engaged, like the classroom teacher, in helping students to understand cause-and-effect relationships. He would have to be able to explain clearly to each student the relative difficulty of each course and the student's demonstrated competence for it. He would also have to be prepared (and I can't overstress the importance of this point in all of our interpersonal relationships) to keep straight accounts of the performance of each of his coun-

selees, but to *keep his books open,* so that a failure at one time could be
made good by success at some later time. He would have to make this clear
to his counselees, and then stand aside to let them choose for themselves,
later assigning them to the classes of their choice and then waiting to see
what happens.

Because this could result in something that looked like a track system,
as failing students were reassigned to less demanding classes, note that
there is a critical difference: each student would be deciding for himself
which courses he wanted to try, and testing the strength of his interest and
motivation against the amount of work required for the course. Against our
expectations, I think, some would succeed, the strength of their interest
enabling them to mobilize and use to advantage more energy than they had
ever shown before. In line with our expectations, others would fail; but
again one failure, in what students themselves had chosen to attempt,
would not leave them forever defeated. They might try again the next year,
or they might change course, but in any case they would be more knowl-
edgeable than before about themselves *vis-à-vis* the kinds of work they
might later do well and happily.

It should be noted also, at least in passing, that to abrogate or even
abridge the right of educators to choose for themselves how they will function, and how they will not, can limit their productivity in just the same
way that denying students the right to choose their courses can limit the
students' productivity; but our right to choose should always be contingent
upon our willingness to accept the consequences of our choices and upon
our ability to learn from experience. In advocating that students should be
given a right to choose their courses, I am simply hoping that a few educators here and there will be willing to experiment with such a practice, to
determine if in fact this kind of school-time sampling of possible careers
would increase students' productivity by promoting more good matches
between each individual and his work.

We need now to consider in somewhat more detail the expectations that
should go along with freedom of choice if we are to help children to achieve
and maintain an optimal level of productivity. It is important to distinguish
here between "optimal" and "maximal." Optimal productivity is maximal
productivity only when considered from the standpoint of the life span. It is
not maximal productivity at all times. People who "function up to capacity" day after day and year after year risk physical and psychological bank-
ruptcy. You have only to read the newspapers regularly to realize how
many phenomenally productive people die young. In the context of our
theory, they spent their energy prodigally until there was no more left to
spend.

But there are empirical findings to support the theory. For example, Johnson, in a study discussed by Reichert, found that junior high school boys worked harder in competitive athletics, but that their output was not significantly greater, and in some cases was less, than that of boys engaged in noncompetitive sports. In addition, the competitive boys showed slower recovery from heart and blood-vessel strain and greater tendency to nausea than the control group. On the basis of these and other similar findings, Reichert concluded that children develop best, physically, by "a process of gradual training," rather than by "the forced development of special skills" (16). Similarly, for another example, Sarason and his colleagues, studying children's academic learning, found that high anxiety yielded high-level performance in rote kinds of learning, but low anxiety yielded superior performance in the more complex learning situations (22). The evidence clearly suggests that forced growth heightens tension and anxiety, and unremitting high tension and high anxiety are corrosive to health, both physical and mental. Again, asking too much too soon of children is hurtful to them.

So, however, is asking too little too late. I have seen no published research on the issue, but I suspect from what some educators have told me that many (not necessarily all) of our ungraded primaries have fallen into this second kind of trap. The ideal of the ungraded primary, to enable young children to learn, each at the pace best suited to him, is beyond reproach. But there is a very common misunderstanding that the pace best suited to each child is the pace that each would choose for himself, and while this will serve well enough for the self-starters and the strugglers, the children who are motivated to learn, it does nothing for the nonstrugglers and the rebels, who (like many adults) produce only as much as is expected or required of them. Where nothing more is expected or required than they are willing to produce, these children will achieve less than they would in graded classes where there are set expectations and requirements. The fact is that as long as we have children who are not motivated to learn, and as long as student-teacher ratios are high, to abandon the stair-step arrangement of grade levels is to lock out of the schools one of the most potent forces for stimulating productivity, namely, the pleasure of climbing, step by step, higher and higher.

Please recognize that this is *not* endorsing without question or reservation the curricula that may be attached to the various grade levels; these should be kept always subject to continuing scrutiny, and evaluated and revised in the light of social change and increasing knowledge. It is simply making the point that, regardless of courses and course content, there is a positive about the stair-step arrangement of grade levels. We may not like to be graded, but we like to be promoted; we like it so well that as adults we find it difficult to resist an offered promotion even when it would bind us to appreciably less congenial tasks. Children like to be promoted, too; they like it so well that even the most play-loving among them are willing to work diligently to earn promotion *if* they understand clearly that they must earn it if they are to get it (30).

One of the keys to eliciting optimal productivity lies in what we call pacing, the process whereby the caretaking adult (parent or teacher or surrogate in this role), watching the child with abiding attentiveness, waits for the signs that he has surplus energy available, and then asks him to produce; and similarly, notes when he is temporarily depleted, and gives him leeway to rest. When you apply this to the issue of maturational readiness, which is of course crucially important to success in the tasks of the early school years, you recognize at once that the maturationally unready child is burdened with homeostatic chores that use up all of his energy. The maturationally ready child can quickly take care of his homeostatic chores, and then is "alive, active, and up to something" (34), and this is the time to ask him to produce. When he is hungry or sleepy or for any reason upset, that is the time to lessen what you ask of him.

This is easy to say, and hard to do. I have known young parents who were able to manage it beautifully with their first child, until the second child was born, at which time it became twice as difficult; and if it becomes twice as difficult again with each additional child, how can any teacher be expected to pace thirty children at a time? There are two ways in which it can be done, one sure, one not so sure.

It is thanks to having watched a young fourth-grade teacher in her first two years of teaching that I know about the not-so-sure way. The young woman was full of bubble and bounce. She liked children and teaching, she had a lively sense of fun and a remarkable sensitivity. She kept her class working hard until some (and to me imperceptible) increase in tension in the children got to her, whereupon she would suddenly remember a joke to tell them, or would jump up and go into a clowning dance, provoking a burst of hilarity, releasing the tension on waves of laughter. Then she might either swing them back to finish the assigned task, or she might say, "Let's quit this for today, we can finish it tomorrow. Let's do something different now." Her students' productivity in her first year of teaching was fully double that of their fourth-grade peers in other classrooms. But she became engaged that year, and by the time the next school year began she was married. She was still conscientious and hard working, but she was not sensitive to the children in the way she had been the year before, and her students' achievement that year was only a little higher than that of their peers in other classrooms. My inference is that the change in her personal life (which was good, but was nevertheless change) kept her working to establish a new equilibrium for herself, and used up the surplus energies that had earlier enabled her to be so intuitive about her class.

Since our personal lives have a way of changing and therefore of making varying demands on our energy supplies, it is fortunate that there is another way open to us. We can use a surplus of energy at any time to plan ahead, to develop a systematic kind of pacing. Two of the ablest administrators I have known applied a pacing technique to recesses. First-graders had half-hour recesses, second-graders had twenty-five minutes, third-graders twenty minutes, and from fourth grade on through sixth grade there were fifteen-minute recesses. Faye Anastasoff, that first-grade teacher mentioned earlier, who teased her students into learning, planned her teaching day in a similarly thoughtful and systematic manner. She expected more of the students at the start of the day, when most of them—if they were not always fresh—at least were fresher than they were likely to be through the rest of the day. She shortened the work periods, and changed activity more frequently as the day progressed, and permitted the children increasing freedom to talk and move about the room as they fatigued toward the end of the day. And productivity in her classes was regularly far above that of other first-grade classes in the same school.

This kind of planned pacing cannot, of course, suit exactly the needs of both the most energetic and the least energetic children in a classroom, but it is a sound technique for teachers to fall back on whenever they find themselves unable to offer individual pacing to each child. (The ideal of "individualized instruction" seems to me to be realistically unattainable for public schools, in any foreseeable future; but I suggest that we should find it less urgent to individualize instruction if we would only take care to individualize *children*.)

The positive principle to be kept in mind is that, other things being equal, productivity tends to generate more productivity. The more we produce, the better we come to like producing and the more we strive to enlarge our capacity to produce. If we can learn to pace children through their growing years, asking more of them when they are able to cope and less of them when they are not, I think we shall find them entering adulthood with levels of productivity that are both high and solid.

Robert Morse recently predicted that "in the not-too-distant future" we shall have a society in which the élite will do all the work, with automation taking over all the work now being done by our labor forces. He points out that even now people in the professions and in topflight managerial positions do twice as much work as they used to do (14). We do not have to commit ourselves to fulfillment of that prediction in order to glean from it the real essence of what I have taken so long to say here: that in the world of work the élite are now, have always been, and always will be those who are in love with their work, wedded to it, and productive in it, those who have recaptured in their maturity the absorbed delight that they felt as children in playing at work and working at play.

Responsibility

If you had a question, as we discussed interpersonal relationships, as to why all talk of dependability was related to parents, and none of it to children, we can answer that question now. While it often happens, and is sometimes unavoidable and necessary, that parents depend upon their children *before* the aging of both has brought about that reversal of roles noted earlier, it is not generally appropriate or good for adults to depend upon children. Dependencies and dependabilities belong in the field of our close interpersonal relationships. The counterpart term, in the field of our work, is responsibility. Let me put it this way: I feel concern for any child who is expected to be dependable in order to meet some adult's dependency needs. Children who are coerced into becoming prematurely dependable are likely to grow up with their own dependency needs largely unmet, and these complicate and distort, if they do not invade and ruin, all of their subsequent personal relationships. On the other hand, however, I would expect a good parent to help his child to become increasingly responsible year by year—for his behavior, his safety, the fulfillment of tasks assigned to him, and the fulfillment of all appropriate interpersonal obligations, particularly those with his peers.

Because responsibility covers the whole spectrum of our moral values, whatever they may be, there is probably no single aspect of human living that gives more people more trouble than this one. It feels so onerous, it seems always so much giving and so little getting, that all of us probably spend more effort and energy in trying to dodge it than in trying to carry it. Many people are willing to work very hard to achieve power or authority or prestige, because all of these things bring gratifying rewards. The only obvious consequence attached to becoming responsible is the dubious privilege of being expected to be even more responsible.

Earlier, in beginning this discussion of how our work might become our proof of worth, I suggested that the first work of our surplus energies is play, and that we begin to distinguish work from play only when society, insisting upon trying to socialize us, requires us to do things that we don't want to do or when we don't want to do them. I think we have to come down hard now on the fact that society is not being very effective in its socializing efforts. Our divorce rates, juvenile delinquency rates, and crime rates long ago reached and passed appalling levels and continue to rise. Neither in homes and families nor in schools is a sense of responsibility being firmly implanted in all or even most children; and I suggest that this is because all of us, children and adults, basically conceive of "society" as *everybody else, collectively bent on hedging me in, abrogating my freedom, and overruling my autonomy.* True, many of us dutifully go to the polls and vote from time to time, and more of us pay taxes (though not because we like to), and we call this being good citizens. But these same actions provide us with scapegoats to blame for our social ills: our elected officials make ridiculous laws, and our tax-paid police are always there to make arrests for minor infractions, but are nowhere in sight when crimes are being committed. (And how many of us have ever made or ever expect to make a citizen arrest? That is not *our* responsibility. *We* are not police.)

We pay a lot of lip service to the value of being responsible, but put almost no thought and effort into really conceptualizing it, let alone into questioning how to actualize it. We wouldn't dream of espousing a "to hell with responsibility" attitude, but we have accepted the track system in schools, in effect establishing an educational horse race in which all that is important, to our vested interests, is who crosses the finish line first, who is in the pack, and who is bringing up the rear. Little merit is attached to running the whole course, although that would constitute evidence of full responsibility.

We are sophisticated enough to know that responsibility is something more than mere submission to authority, or conformity to rules; but we behave as if it could be taken for granted that children will acquire a sense of responsibility quite naturally in the process of growing up, which is nonsense. It is far easier and more natural to remain irresponsible than to launch into the deliberate, focused, and long-sustained effort necessary to become responsible. Take us by and large, we have not accepted responsibility for helping children to become responsible. In fact, most of us have two contracts with the world around us, one public, and the other private, with its terms known only to each of us alone.

This is duplicity; and if we are to clear ourselves of it, we shall have to inquire into the terms of our private contracts. Sometimes they are simple, as when in driving we exceed the speed limit because we feel sure we can get by with it. Sometimes they are not simple. For example, twice a year on my vacation trip I drive through a large city on Saturday morning or Sunday afternoon, when traffic is heavy. They are fine, broad expressways that I travel, three lanes for each direction, and a speed limit of fifty miles an hour. When I observe the speed limit, traffic piles up behind me, drivers' tempers flare, and they blast their horns and weave in and out, seeking to pass me on left or right. I am a traffic hazard, in excellent position to precipitate an accident. When I accelerate to sixty or sixty-five miles an hour, the jam behind me clears away, and traffic flows smoothly, serenely, and far more safely. I have yet to see any police along that road, and in their absence I protect myself and others as best I can, by going illegal.

In the matter of observing laws, in the absence of police, most of us exercise far more autonomy then we publicly admit to. But there is an underlying dilemma to be dealt with. If we are going to encourage children in independence of thinking, in the spirit of inquiry, in the use of good judgment, in the capacity and willingness to be a change-agent—in short, to become productive in the broadest social sense, then we must acknowledge that implicitly we are also encouraging them to challenge some existing laws and to flout some social mores. Moreover, it is they, and not we, who will decide which laws to challenge and which mores to flout, and here, I think, is one of our hang-ups. This is the prospect that scares us into weaseling, into talking about our public contracts as if they were the only contracts we had, or into feeling so guilty about our private contracts that we choose to ignore the issue altogether.

There are only two honest alternatives open to us. Either we exercise autonomy and accept the risk of being penalized if caught in an unsanctioned act, or we surrender as much of our autonomy as we must to conform at all points with existing laws and mores. Before we can begin to make this clear to children, we shall have to become unequivocally clear on the point ourselves: in the field of behavior, learning cause-and-effect relationships depends upon interpersonal experience, specifically, on the capacity and willingness of authority figures to provide appropriate effects (which means meaningful effects) for given causes. All of us as children have operated on the primitive logic that anything is all right if we can get by with it; and we move beyond that primitive logic only if there are people, whose approval is important to us, who refuse to let us get by with certain kinds of behavior—who, in short, provide discipline for us until such time as we are able and willing to discipline ourselves.

But here we encounter another hang-up. When we discussed discipline in the context of developing competence, it was as something that could be and probably better would be quite impersonal. The school requires certain kinds of competencies in children, and the teacher has only to use the best disciplinary strategies available to help the children meet those requirements. But discipline in the context of teaching acceptable behavior is inescapably personal. The school may set certain basic minimal requirements for behavior, but it leaves to classroom teachers a large uncharted area that the teachers themselves must chart in accordance with what each considers acceptable or unacceptable behavior. Now any time we undertake, as people in positions of authority, to impose our values on other people, we are taking on a sizable responsibility, with a proportionate amount of room for error. Since we all like to be well regarded, it is hardly to be wondered at that so many of us prefer to shirk this responsibility than to fulfill it and run the risk of incurring resentment and—even worse—discovering later that we had been in the wrong.

But shirking is not an acceptable out, and so it behooves us to learn how we can become effectively responsible in dealing with children's behavior. Several steps are involved. First, we must be clear about our own values as of today, while recognizing that they are susceptible to change in the light of increasing experience. Second, we must be highly selective in what we propose to make the rules of the house, keeping in mind the difficulty of enforcing them consistently. Then we must learn how to match effect to antecedent cause in the ways that will best enable children to learn from experience. And finally, we shall have to expect to make some mistakes and to be prepared to apologize for them, which is not really a horrendous prospect. Let me fill in this outline by giving you some examples culled from my observations of Lois Kardell, formerly principal of a large and mushrooming school in St. Louis County. I think she would be pleased with this kind of memorial. I am not recommending that anyone else should try to do exactly what she did, because I doubt that anyone else could achieve the same impeccable results that she achieved; but I think that we can learn from her and adapt the learning to our own individual styles.

To begin with, she liked children, perhaps most particularly the feisty little boys who baffled and exasperated most other women. She had dignity and strength in unmistakable degree, but even when she was at her surest, there was a lurking twinkle in her eyes, which was equally unmistakable. The twinkle disappeared whenever she found herself in the wrong and felt called upon to apologize to a child; that she always did with soberly regretful eyes. And I remember one occasion when she apologized to a weeping child in front of a whole first-grade classroom. She said afterward: "You can be sure that I don't make mistakes like that on purpose, but when I do, the public apology has its uses. Teaches the children that grown-ups can make mistakes, too, and had better be ready to apologize when they do."

I went into her outer office early one morning and found two big fellows there, shaking hands with each other, up and down and up and down, struggling not to laugh, but looking very foolish indeed. She looked up from her desk in the inner office and motioned me in, meanwhile explaining, "They were fighting on the playground. I told them that good sports always shake hands after a fight, and since they still had fifteen minutes before the first bell rings, they'll have plenty of time to learn good sportsmanship."

Another time I was in her office when six junior high boys were sent to her because they had been throwing chalk all around the classroom. She looked them over thoughtfully, shaking her head, and said: "Every one of you knows that I like to see boys have fun. You surprise me, thirteen and fourteen years old as you are, that you want to play like six-year-olds, but I guess if that's the way you want it, that's the way we'd better arrange it. Report here every morning next week at 7:45. Bring chairs from the kindergarten, and arrange them in the office out there, three opposite three. I'll have three pieces of new chalk for you, and you can toss them back and forth until the first bell rings. You'll feel pretty foolish, I expect, but then you should have felt pretty foolish in the classroom just now, and you didn't, so you've got a good deal to learn."

In all such arrangements she remained approachable. The two boys who were shaking hands stuck it out until the bell rang; but the chalk-throwers chose a spokesman after the second morning, and presented themselves to her on the third morning, their faces red while their spokesman told her that they had learned, and if she would let them off now, they would promise never to throw chalk again anywhere. She said gravely, "Too much is too much, isn't it? Well, then, we'll call it enough." No gratitude was ever more heartfelt than the thanks the six boys gave her before they went racing out of the building. She swung around in her chair to watch them head across the street, and when they looked back toward her office, she smiled and lifted her hand to them, and they waved their arms wildly, all smiles in response.

She was smooth as silk in working with parents whose children were failing academically, but who angrily demanded that the children be promoted anyhow. She graciously agreed to grant the desired social promotion if the parents would merely sign a simple statement that they accepted full responsibility for the educational outcome. Parents who always before had blamed the school for their childrens' difficulties became more responsible parents under that principal's tutelage, as their children became more responsible children.

What all good disciplinarians have in common with Lois Kardell is a crystal-clear perception that responsibility is the fair price to pay for autonomy. This is the first part of making clear the terms of the alternatives. It is also the point at which the linkage occurs between responsibility, on the one hand, and competence and productivity, on the other hand. The more competent and productive an individual is, the more likely he is to insist on exercising a considerable degree of autonomy, and the more likely he is to have the stamina both to maintain his autonomy and to pay the price of responsibility attached to it. The less competent and productive he is, the more readily will he yield much of his autonomy and abide by the decisions of others, either the authority figures in his world or the consensus of his fellows. Most of us, however, will make the one kind of bargain at some times, and the other kind at other times, with the determination depending in part on the importance of the issue involved, but always more saliently on the ratio of needed energy to available energy at the time. We should be rash to judge anyone's coping strengths by the kind of bargain that he makes at any particular time, unless we know also what other stresses he is having to cope with at the same time.

But if we limit ourselves to bargaining for autonomy, we miss the very positive contribution that reponsibility can make to our psychological economy. There is a whole world of difference between acting responsibly in certain situations and being a fully responsible person, and the difference is a matter of commitment. As long as we harbor any reluctance to accept responsibility, we have to weigh the pros and cons, the possible advantages against the possible disadvantages, of every situation that involves responsibility; and such making of decisions one at a time and each on its own merits uses up enormous quantities of energy. To become fully responsible people we have to dispense with bargaining, and simply commit ourselves once and for all to making it part of our way of life to be responsible.

At first thought this may seem like buying an undetermined and indeterminable amount of stress, sight unseen; but second thought will reveal that it is almost the polar opposite of that. To assume more responsibility than is appropriately our own *and within our current ability to discharge successfully* is to be just as irresponsible as to assume no responsibility at all. I think we generally recognize that we insidiously undermine the strength of others when we take over their responsibilities (unless they are in real need of temporary help). It is not quite so easy to see that we hurt others, as well as ourselves, when we fail to recognize that sometimes our own responsibilities are more than we can handle alone at the time—when we start out bravely enough, but then bog down, and either the task goes undone, or someone else has to come and finish it for us.

Committing ourselves to be responsible is the basic decision. It does not relieve us of all subsequent decision-making, but it does free us to generalize from one situation to others like it, and in the pinch to make subsequent decisions in the rational terms of "I can" or "I can't," instead of in the conflicted terms of "Should I?" or "Shouldn't I?" or—in the most surely disaster-inviting terms of all—"Well, dammit, I don't want to, but I guess I have to." Once we have settled the more primitive conflict and resolved the basic issue by unqualified commitment, we are launched into a process that will lead in time to a hierarchical ordering of our other commitments on the basis of their relative importance to us. For one person religion may come first, family second, work third, health fourth. For another, work may come first, health second, family third, and religion fourth. But whatever the arrangement of the priorities, the development of an order in them not only frees more large quantities of energy, but also produces a feeling of internal balance and security. It is as if each such deliberately ordered priority anchors and steadies and helps to nourish us as roots anchor and steady and help to nourish a tree. Some loss of flexibility is necessarily involved, a fact that should alert us to being as thoughtful as possible in the ordering process; but once you have experienced the clean economy of this kind of transaction, you no longer question whether responsibility can be a psychosocial resource. It still calls for work, but for work commensurate with our strength to carry out, and rich in the double reward of bringing us peace of mind about ourselves and about our relations with all of our significant Others.

A Note on Teachers and Teaching

Throughout this discussion of our work as "proof of worth" there has been much talk of schools and of teachers and of how they can help children to grow toward competence, productivity, and responsibility. But we have not talked about one matter that ought to concern us all, namely, the fact that so many thoroughly competent, productive, and responsible teachers habitually overestimate what they should do, and underestimate what they actually do. As a result their work is not a psychosocial resource to them to the degree that it could and should be.

There are two obvious reasons for the problem, and one that is not so obvious. The obvious ones are, first, that our society does not accord teachers either the pay or the status commensurate with the responsibility that it delegates to them, and second, that teachers are constantly being prodded, by practically everyone in sight, to do more than it is realistically possible for anyone to do, but they try, and they fail, and then they feel inadequate. The not so obvious reason is that most teachers, like most other professionals, also have family obligations, and they are almost bound to be caught from time to time in coinciding peak demands from both work and family. Under such circumstances it becomes difficult to view either our work or our families as psychosocial resources; both seem like psychosocial burdens.

But if you look at how we tend to operate under such conditions, a different picture emerges. Suppose, for example, that you have someone at home who is seriously ill. You arrange for daytime care, so that you can meet your work obligations, but you have either to offer the nighttime care yourself or at least share it. And your anxiety and distress mount through the night, hour by hour, and you long for morning to come, and when it finally does come and brings your relief, you rush to your job and plunge into work. You don't forget about the patient at home, but at least you are primarily occupied with other things, until toward the end of the working day you can suddenly no longer bear to be away from home. We are in flight twice a day during times like these, fleeing away from home in the morning, fleeing back to home at night; but the respite thus gained during the day is often all that makes it possible for us to handle the nighttime vigil and nursing care. Our anxiety would reach intolerable heights if we had no way to interrupt it periodically. If in this way our work gives us staying power, a capacity to wait out stress without being overwhelmed by it, then our work is obviously a very real resource.

But this is still looking at the matter rather negatively, and there is a positive way of looking at it as well. Teachers will never be as effective in their teaching as they can be until they can delight in the use of their skills, as well as in the response that these skills elicit from their students. And since the first step toward delighting in one's skill is recognizing that it is a skill, and a lot of teachers are unaware of their own skills (perhaps because we so seldom offer them the mirrors of our perceptions), I want to set out here in somewhat global terms what *I* think it is that makes a teacher good. Let me postulate an enlightened administration that permits each teacher to develop her own individual style; there is no single "right way" to do it—there are multitudinous "right ways." And though I am going to follow the convention of speaking of the teacher as "she," this is only to avoid the awkwardness of having to say "he or she" every time there is need to use a pronoun. What I have to say applies just as well to men as to women.

First, a good teacher is a highly sensitive camera. She focuses on child after child, until she has captured and fixed in her memory an eloquent likeness of every child in the class. She will not rest content with getting mere stereotypes. Wiener says about communication, "The more probable the message, the less information it gives" (35), and the same thing is true of photographs; it is the rare, the unexpected, the often fleeting expression on a child's face that tells us something new and additional about him, that helps the teacher to discern in him more than the child himself knows is there. What he does know, though, and what he is going to respond to, as positively as he is capable of responding, is that here is someone who looks at him with eyes that seem to see something special in him; and nothing is more conducive to growth than this kind of quiet, abiding, interested attentiveness.

At the same time a good teacher uses herself as a skilled photographer uses a fine camera, bringing the subject matter into clear focus free from distracting irrelevancies around and about it. If you have ever asked yourself why you notice in a good movie things that you had seen repeatedly in your own life without noticing, you will know that it is because the camera has focused your attention, giving you first, perhaps, a broad landscape in which no detail seemed particulary important, but then moving closer, narrowing the focus, until finally you notice the one particular thing you were meant to notice. This is the fine art of photography, and this is the fine art of good teaching. The teacher will "shoot the scene," as it were, from different angles, odd and intriguing, funny and surprising, and then move to something else that is mystifying at first, disturbing and suspenseful because it seems unrelated, but little by little gaining significance as the camera does its work, until at last it is seen as satisfyingly relevant to the first subject, as indeed indispensable to full understanding.

When I spoke of the importance of entertaining children, much earlier in this discussion, I mentioned the two modes of entertaining, and emphasized the quieter one of welcoming children into the classroom. Our concern there was more for the children than for their teachers. Here, where our concern is more for the teachers and their learning how to make their work as rich a psychosocial resource as it can be, I want to stress the other kind of entertaining, the active kind. In entertaining others, if we do it effectively, we also entertain ourselves. Teachers capable of amusing children are themselves at the same time amused; and exactly as children learn with astonishing ease and quickness, given a teacher with a light touch and lively sense of fun, so are the teacher's own skills quickly and easily elaborated and refined by her amusement. If I were limited to saying just one thing to teachers, in the hope of helping them to become better teachers, to their own benefit as well as to that of their students, it would be simply: Have fun!

Chapter 5. THE FOURTH PSYCHOSOCIAL RESOURCE

Candleflames have a fascinating attribute: as long as they are alight, they can give light to any number of other candles that may then be carried off in any number of different directions. Personalities and psychological equipment and ideas have the same attribute, too. Long years ago, in the course of a diagnostic staff conference on a patient, our young psychiatrist said: "This woman has absolutely no capacity for pleasure." And suddenly I found myself with a new light burning bright and clear —the conviction that the capacity for pleasure was an indispensable component of mental health.

Nothing that has happened since then has made that light waver even momentarily, although—as you will soon see—our interpretation of the concept has undergone great change over the intervening years. To begin with, the term *pleasure* often carries an implication of license; and although for a while this seemed to have a certain shock value in working with teachers, eliciting immediate and alert attention, any implication of license was obviously in ill accord with the other three psychosocial resources that we were delineating. So I substituted the more innocent term *enjoyment,* which could be easily confined within the limits set by the other three dimensions. This at once suggested a cryptogram of mental health—and posed a further difficulty.

On the one hand, a cryptogram could serve to meet one of our criteria for good guidelines, specifically that they should be simple enough to be readily grasped and easily kept in mind; and I was further encouraged by the statement of Dr. Thomas Gold that rapid progress in the sciences will come not only from technical advances by scientists, but also from the simplification of their underlying principles to the point where these become "common school-boy knowledge" (8). On the other hand, while I tend to believe that if I cannot somehow diagram a concept, I have not really thought it through, this cryptogram had seemed to shape itself, and I had by no means really thought it through, and therefore it could be erroneous, which would automatically make it unusable for teaching purposes.

My conflict about it was finally resolved when recently, and belatedly, I came across an engaging and illuminating piece by John Platt, entitled "Beauty: Pattern and Change" (19). A small part of it is an elegantly simple illustration of Wiener's statment that "the more probable the message, the less information it gives" (25). If, Platt says, one draws a figure like this:

and stops there, we feel a mild discomfort. We want closure. Closure is easily gained by simply completing the circle, so:

that is that and the figure is of no further interest.

Suppose, however, that instead of completing the circle, we leave it incomplete, but add a mirror image of it, like this:

We have now achieved symmetry, which yields another kind of satisfaction; but we have twice as much need as before for closure, and our interest is somewhat heightened by suspense. If we make the obvious move, to gain closure without losing the symmetry, we can complete both circles:

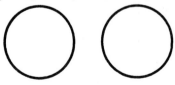

but this is almost annoying. The bit of suspense that was piqued by adding a mirror image of the incomplete circle has collapsed just as we had begun to enjoy it. We have pattern (symmetry and closure), but no interest whatsoever. (Hans Selye, incidentally, makes precisely this point in relation to insomnia, saying that it is suspense and incompleteness that keeps us awake at night, and that the best way to insure oneself a good night's sleep is to make a point of achieving completeness in some area of the day's activities (20).)

But Platt's concern was to bring into clear focus the basic elements of a satisfying design, which call not only for pattern and symmetry and closure, but also for something unexpected, and so he goes back to the two incomplete circles:

and attains his aim by superimposing a third circle in such a way that as it closes itself, it also closes the other two:

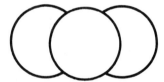

Notice that at each of the three steps in this process Platt has considered the "more probable" message, and then rejected it in favor of the less probable, and in this way has increased both the fun of the game and its yield of information. Take my cryptogram as a similar kind of game, giving me leave to alter it whenever new evidence or better logic demand some alteration, and it can then be offered in good conscience for whatever it may be worth.

If our formulations up to this point have validity, then good interpersonal relationships is the basic psychosocial resource. Self-esteem emerges out of the interpersonal matrix, as the child absorbs into his beginning sense of self the love that others, particularly his parents, show toward him. But it seems obvious that self-esteem cannot thrive indefinitely on just the approval of other people. Sooner or later it has to be supported by proof of one's worth, by one's becoming competent, productive, and responsible; and this proof of worth in turn feeds into one's interpersonal relationships and enriches them. The diagram that is thus suggested would look like an isosceles triangle with rounded angles, each side representing one of these three mental health dimensions, and the rounded angles suggesting their way of merging into each other so that there is no saying exactly where one ends and another begins. Momentarily we have also what looks like premature closure, ruling out our fourth postulated mental health dimension; but if you recall that the term *enjoyment* was chosen so that it could be fitted into the context of the other three dimensions, the next move is obvious and productive. Put a big E inside the triangle, to represent the fourth resource as operant within the framework of the other three, like this:

And because we usually refer to time when we speak of the fourth dimension, it now becomes a natural to conceive of enjoyment as linked to time, and to growth over time, and thus capable of expanding the whole triangle.

Problems in conceptualization, however, are not so easily solved. Marie Jahoda, the acknowledged pioneer in attempts to define mental health, tried to include "happiness" in her formulation, but could not be satisfied with it because happiness is so dependent on environmental factors; and even if you say, instead, "a capacity for happiness," given appropriate circumstances, this seemed to her to overlap with her other variables, such as self-acceptance, integration, and attempts at environmental mastery (13). Jacob Levine, writing on "Humor and Mental Health" (15), and Martha Wolfenstein, in her book *Children's Humor* (26), are both more concerned with the defensive, anxiety-reducing function of humor than with its potential for promoting growth through enjoyment. Moreover, probably all of us know a number of people who seem reasonably solid in the other three factors that we have been discussing, but are quite lacking in enjoyment. There was thus good reason to question whether enjoyment is really indispensable to growth in the other three dimensions, and if it is not so indispensable, would it not perhaps be more accurate to view it as the hallmark of mental health, a manifestation rather than a component?

We have to look to research for answers to questions like those, but the answers are forthcoming only if the research puts some theory to test. In the summer of 1962 we were preparing to start a series of research interviews with several hundred mothers, focusing on the patterns of psychosocial growth in children. If we could find some way to assess enjoyments, the opportunity was at hand to determine if and how enjoyment might be related to mental health. The question was how to go about assessing enjoyments.

I had had a disheartening experience a few months earlier, when I asked a group of educators to respond to the challenge, "Name me three things that have given you, today, a moment of pure enjoyment." The group sat in stunned silence; and silence was still the response when I asked for just two things; even one thing. And yet that fiasco seemed irrelevant to the thing that I was reaching for, partly out of intuition and partly out of experience.

There are games that make enjoyment more enjoyable by making it more specific. For example, on long vacation drives we might spend hours in trying to choose the five most beautiful things we had ever seen, or the five most beautiful things we had ever heard, or smelled or tasted or touched. We might vary the game at times to try to decide which five books or five records or five paintings we would choose if we could have only five of each for the rest of our lives. In a somewhat similar vein a bright young first-grade teacher told me that she regularly left the last ten minutes of the school day for the children to answer the question, "What was fun today?" and she added that she learned from this more about the children and about how best to teach them than from anything else that she did. One of Fran Porter's most popular parlor games was to hand out slips of paper to her guests and ask them to list the three character traits that they most admired in others and would like best to have in themselves; then the papers were folded, shuffled, and redistributed, the challenge being to see how many people could be identified by the three traits they had listed. Surely the same ploy could be used in a game of favorite enjoyments, perhaps with some hilarious results.

There are solitary games, too, that can be illuminating. One is to list all of your remembered enjoyments, by the various stages of your life. (This one, incidentally, yielded so short a list for the years of my adolescence that it raises an unanswerable question: Would I have had so hard a time producing a long list when I was still in my teens, or is it only in looking back on those years that they seem so poor in enjoyments?) Another is to sort out from among your current enjoyments those that you have discovered for yourself, and those that you have learned from others, and specifically from whom. There is a rather devastating counterpart to that question, and we might do well to ask it of ourselves more frequently than we do. It is: What enjoyment have I given someone else today?

Out of this kind of questioning there was finally developed an Enjoyments Checklist of thirty items for our research interview schedules, ten items having to do (we hoped) with interpersonal relationships, ten with intrapersonal items, perhaps related to self-esteem, and ten with competence, productivity, and responsibility. The Enjoyments Checklist was to be a structured ending of the interview, and our psychiatric caseworkers were under instructions to start each interview with the same tip-off question, "What about this child have you found most interesting?" Although all of the mothers to be interviewed would be volunteers for the study, it could be assumed that they would volunteer out of a number of different kinds of motivations; and we had hoped to obtain better interviews (less defensive, more open) by giving them opportunity to start talking about positives in their children.

More than half of the mothers, however, were unable to answer the tip-off question. They had not been used to thinking of their children as *interesting. Good* or *bad,* yes, or *disappointing* or *gratifying,* yes, but *interesting?* They were at a loss until given the probe "—or perhaps most concerning?" Then they could talk. As the caseworkers began to report on their interviews, we began to think that the mothers rather sorted themselves into three different groups. There was a group of dutiful but somewhat unloving mothers who tended to report that their children "regularly" or "enthusiastically" enjoyed almost all of the thirty items on the Checklist, but did it so glibly that it sounded to the caseworkers like denial. Then there was a group of loving mothers who so clearly enjoyed their children, and enjoyed talking about them, that the caseworkers were fully persuaded that they did in fact have children with many enjoyments.

The third group of mothers reacted to the Enjoyments Checklist with dismay, either because they found that they knew very little about what their children enjoyed, or because they suddenly realized that their children seemed to have little or no enjoyment of anything. They were not merely left dismayed, however, because in the very process of going through the Checklist they gained clues as to what they could do to improve the situation. The caseworkers reported that many of them left the interview with a look of new purpose, and with verbalizations ranging all the way from a simple "I'm going to do something about this" to "It's bad enough to realize that I have a child who isn't enjoying much. It's even worse to discover that I haven't been enjoying my child. I'm going straight home to wait for him, and when he comes, I'm just going to look at him and love him with my eyes and begin to enjoy him again." Clearly these were loving mothers, but they had become so ensnared in the concerns of child training that all enjoyment had drained out of them.

Whether or not those particular mothers and their children gained in enjoyment through its having been called to their attention, we do not know; but it is relevant to add here that about a year after I had challenged the group of educators to name three things that they had enjoyed that day, I had a chance encounter with one woman from the group, who stopped me to say: "I learned a lesson that day. I thought I was a person who had a pretty good time living, but I was appalled to realize that if I had enjoyed anything that day, I couldn't recall it. Since then, I've paid attention, and I just wanted you to know that I think I've experienced more pure enjoyment since then than I had in all my fifty years before." In one woman, at least, bringing the concept into clear focus, calling attention to it in ways that were both implicitly and explicitly sanctioning, had by her own testimony significantly and permanently enhanced her enjoyments. If we could find that this happened with any regularity, then it could fairly be claimed that enjoyment was not merely a manifestation of mental health, but was in fact its growth-generating component.

Our project in early detection was not designed to yield empirical data on that point; but it brought further support for the findings of other investigators connecting mental health, interpersonal skills, self-esteem, and achievement (7), and it added enjoyment as another highly significant variable. To put it in the terms I used earlier, we found that our "self-starters" scored high on all dimensions, but were conspicuously high in self-esteem, in enjoyment, and in C-P-R. Our "nonstrugglers" were conspicuously low in C-P-R, our "rebels" were conspicuously low in C-P-R and in interpersonal relationships, and our "strugglers" were conspicuously low in everything except C-P-R (that is, low in interpersonal relationships, in self-esteem, and in enjoyment) (21). Those findings make sense, we think, but they are still open to challenge on the basis that our caseworkers were rating the children within the framework of this particular mental health theory, which links the four psychosocial resources to mental health and therefore would automatically produce high intercorrelations between them.

In a subsequent project entitled "Mothers as Colleagues in School Mental Health Work" (22), focusing on children from the time they entered Kindergarten until they completed Grade II, we again asked mothers to volunteer for individual research interviews, using the same interview schedule as before. This time, however, two caseworkers in turn observed in each of the project classrooms long enough to complete an observation schedule for every child in the room *before* the research interviews with their mothers took place. The observation schedule was a guesswork kind of thing (from first to last the formulation of theory lagged far behind the needs of our research), and the ten items on the Enjoyments Scale bore little resemblance to the thirty items of the Enjoyments Checklist of the research interview schedules. Nevertheless, the classroom observations yielded caseworker ratings for each child in all four of our postulated psychosocial resources, as well as in overall mental health status. We were thus able to divide the children into four mental health groups according to caseworker ratings on the basis of observation, and then later to look at the research interview schedules to determine how their mothers had responded to the tip-off question.

Significantly enough, 85 percent of the mothers who were able to respond positively to that question had children whom the caseworkers had placed in the emotionally healthier categories, while 79 percent of the mothers who could only start with expressions of concern or ambivalence had children who had been assigned to the more disturbed categories (23). Moreover, by comparing the children's Enjoyment ratings on the observation schedules with their mothers' responses to the tip-off question, we found that the mothers who saw their children as "interesting" were significantly more likely to have children with a good capacity for enjoyment than were the mothers who were loving but anxious or the mothers who were dutiful but unloving. There is a missing link here that for the time being can be filled only by an inference—that the mothers who found their children "interesting" also enjoyed their children most of the time, and children who feel enjoyed are likely to be children with a good capacity for enjoying.

We have some tantalizing indications, from our preliminary analyses, not only that enjoyment is an independent variable, but also that the relative influence of each psychosocial resource on children's mental health changes over time, and if these findings hold up under more rigorous scrutiny, they will be good support for our theory. A missing link, however, is always a troublesome thing, and an inference adduced to fill it may all too easily be analogous to the visible part of an iceberg, yielding no clue as to what its shape is underneath the surface of the water. At this point, therefore, we have to turn from our empirical data to search further into whatever it is that we are calling enjoyment.

Since we began with games in the first place, let us begin with games again here. They fall into two broad categories—those in which we ourselves are actively participant, and those where we are spectators only. Both kinds yield their own particular enjoyments. Where we are actively participant, as in the small, friendly game that we share with family or friends or neighbors, the spirit of play is in the ascendant, and we enjoy both our own skills and coups, and the skills and coups of those we play with, and we can laugh both at our own goofs and the goofs of others. Bower makes a further point about such games, proposing (if I heard him correctly) that their liberating effect comes from the fact that they can usually be replayed, so that while we don't expect to be the winner every time, we can always hope to win at some time or times.* Because they are not "for keeps," they are necessarily open-ended, and we move in and out of them freely. Depending upon the kind of game, whether it is chess or bridge or tennis or golf, we invest varying amounts and kinds of energy in them, but we give them all we have, and we finish them feeling physically or intellectually spent but at the same time relaxed and exhilarated.

Where we are spectators, we enjoy vicarious experiences. We identify with the players, or with one selected player or team, and we almost feel in our own muscles the beauty of perfectly executed movements, the grace of a superb skill, and the occasional breathtaking miracle of accomplishing the almost impossible feat. The same thing applies to other kinds of spectator involvements, which we might more appropriately call recipient involvements, as when we read someone else's poetry, listen to someone else's music, watch someone else's dancing. Again we pour considerable energy into such focused attentiveness, and again we end such involvements feeling spent but at the same time refreshed and elated.

Since these delightful after-feelings are not the usual outcome of energy expenditure, but rather the opposite, we have to question what is different here? It looks as if enjoyment is a homeostatic mechanism and one of the finest. At a venture (because we are still exploring) I am going to suggest that it operates as a homeostat in either of two ways, depending upon the circumstances: it can drain off surplus energy that might otherwise keep us in disequilibrium (an obvious example is sexual urgings); or it can drain off, into innocence, feelings like hostility and frustration, which it would be severely energy-depleting to try to contain. Whether or not angry feelings are in fact drained off into innocence depends, of course, upon whether the player's basic intent is really play and enjoyment of play, or in-fighting under the guise of play. Eric Berne's book *Games People Play* (1) lays out in detail many of the latter kind of games, and I mention them here primarily to bear down on one point: that there is nothing that looks so much like black magic as the ease with which we can destroy enjoyment in others, particularly in those who love us. A single disparaging comment will do it;

---

*Personal conversation, March 21, 1968.

and if you need examples, here are a few: "How on earth can you sit in front of that idiot-box and listen to such drivel?" "And how was your bridge-party today, dear?—plenty of juicy gossip, I trust?" "Oh, by all means go golfing. The yard here can't look worse next week than it looks today." "You bought *that* thing to wear tonight? Well, your mother should have known better than to let you go shopping alone."

Comments like these would not be devastating if the issues were religion or politics, and perhaps this is why we can gull ourselves into thinking them harmless even when we know perfectly well that they do exactly what we intend them to do—they kill enjoyment. They do even more: if they are said often enough, they kill not only enjoyment, but self-esteem and aspirations and interpersonal relationships as well. The work is so destructive that it is difficult to see just how ridiculous (as well as hostile) the underlying assumptions are: in simplest translation, What *I* enjoy is worth enjoying, but what *you* enjoy is stupid, which proves that you are stupid, too. The underlying assumptions are unfortunately the only message that invariably comes through, and at very best it alienates. We grow quickly distrustful of killjoys, the people who are willing and able to wipe out our enjoyments, and we put as much distance as possible between them and us.

Fortunately, while enjoyment is easily killed, the capacity to enjoy is tougher and more resilient. It can withstand years of remaining merely a capacity, unfulfilled, and still—given the right conditions—surge up again into vivid experiencing. Millay, in her poem *Renascence,* has captured the difference; with respect to the capacity, like this—

> The world stands out on either side
> No wider than the heart is wide;
> Above the world is stretched the sky,—
> No higher than the soul is high.
> The heart can push the sea and land
> Farther away on either hand;
> The soul can split the sky in two,
> And let the face of God shine through.
> But East and West will pinch the heart
> That cannot keep them pushed apart;
> And he whose soul is flat—the sky
> Will cave in on him by and by.

and with respect to the experiencing, like this—

> And all at once the heavy night
> Fell from my eyes and I could see,—

A drenched and dripping apple-tree,
A last long line of silver rain,
And as I looked a quickening gust
Of wind blew up to me and thrust
Into my face a miracle
Of orchard-breath, and with the smell,—
I know not how such things can be!—
I breathed my soul back into me.*

By these lines and even by mention of the name of the poem they came from, I am trying to alert you to the fact that our fourth psychosocial resource involves much more than games and much more than we commonly mean by the word "enjoyment." It has taken experience to teach me this, specifically, experience in what happens in fairly intensive two-week mental-health workshops when the time comes for what we call "the Enjoyments session." What happens then and what its meaning seems to be, we shall be discussing in some detail a little later. Here I want only to acknowledge that what follows is essentially a distillation of what I have learned from these workshop groups.

About Enjoyment—in Interpersonal Relationships

We like to think of newborns as enjoying the best of creature comforts, the basic ones of being amply fed, softly enwrapped, and contentedly asleep. The fact is, however, that from the moment of birth, from the instant of being ejected from the protecting womb, the newborn is not only exposed to insecurity, but is also subject to the hurt of hunger and the discomfort of being too hot or too cold. The first experience in the world is anything but enjoyment. It is pain and struggle and deprivation, and an infant comes by his creature comforts only as some nurturing adult provides them. His first enjoyment, thus, is a little like the old saw, the question "Why do you keep hitting yourself in the head with that hammer?" and the response "Because it feels so good when I stop." The difference is that the infant himself has no control over either what hurts him or what comforts him. The likeness is that in both situations, that of the infant and that of the tired old joke, enjoyment results from replacing a negative by a positive.

---

*From "Renascence" by Edna St. Vincent Millay. In *Collected Poems*. New York: Harper & Row, 1917. Copyright 1917, 1945 by Edna St. Vincent Millay. By permission of Norma Millay Ellis.

Since the infant is unable to do this for himself, someone else—usually his mother—has to do it for him. So the first enjoyment, for most of us, occurs in an interpersonal relationship, as relief from stress and a dawning sense of well-being, associated with being securely and gently held, in warm bodily contact, in suckling and feeling the empty stomach fill up, and in peacefully drifting off to sleep.

In the course of time, in a matter of weeks, the baby learns to recognize the people whose caretaking brings him these pleasant feelings; and if they come frequently enough, or promptly enough on his demanding cry, he begins to respond to their approach with a smile of dazzling delightedness. This has its effect on his caretakers, and they beam upon him in return; and thus, gradually and by imperceptible degrees, his sense of well-being merges into a feeling of being enjoyed. You can tell when this change comes, because when it does, he no longer falls asleep while nursing. The creature comforts, basic as they are, take second place to the feeling of being enjoyed; and now, when his hunger is allayed, he wants to be played with. He wants an adult head nudging gently into his middle, to the accompaniment of soft growlings, and he bursts into upgushing, burbling, uncontainable laughter while his hands clutch your hair to keep you repeating the play again and again—until his ecstatic laughter sends him into hiccups.

It is hardly possible to overestimate, and all too easy to underestimate, the strength and tenacity of the wish to be enjoyed. It is paramount in our interpersonal relationships from beginning to end. It is the prime motivator in our learning to please, and in the baby's learning to please. By the time he is ready to learn that, he will have a number of other sources of entertainment, in what he can see and what he can do and the noises he can make as well as in the toys he may have, and he can be happy alone in crib or playpen for some time at a stretch; but let anyone come near him without seeming to notice and enjoy him, and all of those other entertainments immediately lose their appeal. Nothing will serve him until he can feel enjoyed again, and his single-minded aim is to beguile that other person into enjoying him. He makes love, he kisses, he pats, he hugs and clings and cuddles, all the while on the *qui vive* to see if he is succeeding in his wooing. The analogy to adult lovemaking is quite clear, the underlying purpose in both cases being to gain (or regain) warm, close, physical, interpersonal intimacy and the double feeling of enjoying and being enjoyed.

Notice how, even at so young an age, the baby's enjoyment begins to nourish his interpersonal relationships. The baby's aim in this kind of interpersonal transaction is purely narcissistic; he is not in the least concerned about how the other person may be feeling in any other respect, as long as the other person is enjoying him. But he can fulfill his aim only by making himself enjoyable and thus in fact contributing to the other person's enjoyment. The process involves the beginning of understanding others. Before he has any words to help him, before he even has much in the way of experiential traces to guide him, he is hard at work trying to discern which of his possible activities can elicit the desired response. He may never put it into words, may never recognize it as understanding, except for a cocky confidence that he knows how to get what he wants from other people. Nevertheless, whenever we learn how to please another person, we have gained some understanding of that person, and this can be the beginning of our ability to relate significantly to others.

Harry and Margaret Harlow, through their work with rhesus monkeys, have illuminated both the significance of the mother-infant relationship, and the significance of play, for the infant's subsequent social adjustment. You may remember the earlier reference to the monkeys who were separated from their mothers at birth and reared in isolation, who became grossly defective adults, unable to mate, and unwilling to mother (9). However, the Harlows also had a group of infants who were separated from their mothers at birth, but reared together, and these showed so little evidence of being permanently and severely damaged as a result of having been deprived of mothering that the Harlows tentatively suggested that "opportunity for optimal infant-infant interaction may compensate for lack of mothering" (10).

To some of us this was an unsettling idea, and it may have been so for the Harlows and their colleagues, too, because they proceeded to further experiments to test the effects of different kinds of mothering. They left some babies with their mothers, but denied them any opportunity to play with other babies; and these "mother-captive" infants showed both extreme wariness and hyperaggressiveness when they were later exposed to monkeys of their own age. Another group of babies they left with their mothers, but they also gave them opportunity to play with other babies of their own age; and these normally mothered infants appeared to develop a strong sense of security in the mother-infant relationship, which then allowed them to move freely and playfully into peer relationships. So the Harlows now suggest that one of the mother's most important functions is to be an infant-surrogate for her infant, to teach him to play and to relate through playing, so that when he has outgrown his infancy he knows how to play with his age-mates and to relate to them through playing (11).

That is not merely a charming suggestion. It deserves to be underscored, learned by heart, printed indelibly on our minds, that one of a mother's most important functions is to play with her baby so that he can learn to play and relate through playing. We have begun to recognize how important the mother-baby communication is to the child's subsequent learning ability (12); because in the beginning that communication is largely nonverbal and therefore one of its primary modes is play, programs are being developed in a few places to teach mothers how to play with their babies. Perhaps it was inevitable, in our work-oriented society, that we should first recognize the importance of play as it relates to learning, but heaven help us if we stop with that! It is not the child's learning alone that is affected by the lack of parent-child play. When we come to study the matter carefully, I think we shall find that the adults who are incapable of forming lasting love relationships, in which they both enjoy and feel enjoyed, had been babies whose parents never played with them in loving and enjoying ways.

We fall so easily into grimness. I used to ask myself, whenever I heard that delightful laughter that comes gushing out of a baby when a loving adult is playing with him, What will happen to that laughter? Where does it go, and when?—because we never seem to notice its going: we simply realize one day that we haven't heard it in a long, long time. Go into almost any kindergarten nowadays and listen: the chances are that you'll hear no laughter there. The children are being readied for first grade. This does not necessarily mean that they have lost their capacity for laughter, but it does mean that they have learned to repress it in the presence of adults, and to save it for the times when they are with their age-mates and free of adult surveillance.

It is not very pleasant to realize how effectively we repress the laughter in children, without (as a rule) really meaning to do so, but we had better face it. We have written and read and said and heard innumerable words about what "a good mother" is and does, and what "a bad mother" is and does, but you have to hunt hard to find anything about what "a fun mother" is and does, or "a fun father" or "a fun teacher." Children could tell us about "fun people," if we bothered to ask them; and if we learned from what they might say, we should have less of a generation gap to worry about.

Even with fun parents, however, the patterns of play and of parent-child relationships change over time. There will be an overlapping phase, a period during which the child swings back and forth between wanting to perpetuate the old love-play with his parents and preferring to play with his own age-mates. But this comes to an end when the child begins to stereotype his parents as part of plowing his primitive dependency needs underground and out of sight and mind. Personal intimacy between child and parent begins to become taboo then, and children look to other children for the more personal and cherished relationships.

The parents then are no longer in themselves the source of the child's enjoyment, but are rather the provider of his enjoyments, some of which they may share—as the picnic or the fishing trip, the games or the hobbies, the intently serious conversations, and the give-and-take challenge of clowning double-talk. It is taken for granted that the parents will continue to provide the creature comforts and as many additional pleasures as it is in their power to bestow, including that still most important one of enjoying the child as he is and as he grows and changes—unless there is someone else in the home (a grandparent, for example) who can enjoy him all the more for not being involved in the prohibiting, the requiring, and the refusing that so regularly touch off youthful rebellion against parents.

Later, when the boy-girl relationships begin to develop, parents are expected to be almost entirely altruistic and to continue to provide for enjoyments that they themselves are not allowed to share. And if this seems like a great deal of giving, and very little receiving in return, keep in mind that it is this kind of imbalance that helps to make it possible for parents to enjoy emancipating their children when the children are ready to be emancipated!

The enjoyments that parents and children can share with each other and find in each other do not end there, though they change in the ways implied in the earlier discussion of the interpersonal network; but I want to make two further points now about interpersonal relationships in general. The first relates to friendships and to the noncontractual relationships that are based on liking, which is enjoying. Friendships develop most frequently and easily between congenial people, whose attitudes and tastes and value systems are much alike. It follows naturally that we enjoy our friends, and they enjoy us, and we and they tend to have the same kinds of other enjoyments; but it also follows that congenial friends rarely add much to each other's *repertory* of enjoyments. We learn new kinds of enjoyments from people who are *not* like us, who find their interests and values and pleasures along paths that we have never explored, and who on their part have never explored the paths most interesting to us. Much of the delight of being a beachcomber or a bird-watcher or a wildflower enthusiast lies in the fact that you start every expedition with the eager, anticipatory question: I wonder what is waiting for me today? Among the people I have known, those who have had the largest repertory of enjoyments are those who approached each new acquaintance with a counterpart question, I wonder what things "turn him on"? what things "send him"?—as Laurie is "sent" by the sight of the first golden crocus in spring or the flight pattern of birds, or as Jennifer is "turned on" by fragrances. When you find answers to this kind of question, and out of curiosity have tried them on for size, you often find that you have discovered a new kind of enjoyment for yourself, and perhaps a new kind of friend as well.

The second point concerns remembering. This may be the major source of enjoyment for the aging person who cannot be actively participant in many things, whose age-mates become fewer each year as they die off, and who may be alone much of the time. But remembered enjoyments are by no means limited to aging people. They are available to all of us from the time when we first become able to remember. Some of us may have to be challenged before we remember our enjoyments, and some of us, so challenged, may discover that we have not really had much enjoyment, which is all the more reason for raising the issue, as I shall be doing throughout this chapter. Let me call your attention, parenthetically, to the intrapersonal enjoyment of remembering: it is remembering that is responsible for most of our happy anticipations. A two-year-old may be dazzled by a lighted and fully bedecked Christmas tree, but the four-year-old who can remember the Christmas before has a month of happy anticipation before he sets eyes on his Christmas tree. Those of us who can remember twenty or thirty or fifty springtimes, or more, know hundreds of harbingers to look for and delight in, because we "learned by heart" all those earlier springtimes. Translating this back into interpersonal terms may make it possible to dispel a common misunderstanding that often beclouds one of the peak experiences in remembered enjoyments.

It happens sometimes that after the death of some well-loved person, family and friends will sit together for long hours, talking and laughing. To many people this is both incomprehensible and repugnant; and it is justifiably so *if* the wake is marked by phobic hilarity, attempting to deny the death and evade the work of mourning. But some wakes are intensely memorial and lit with a brilliance of grief as friends try to retrieve and share every remembered enjoyment, as if they were trimming the wicks of the myriad candles of a life until they all stand with clear and unwavering light, in the people who remember.

There is no way to make the work of mourning anything except hard and lonely work, concerned as it has to be with trying to adapt to loss and change, and sometimes having also to work through regrets and guilt; but it is remembering with enjoyment that lends brilliance to grief, just as it is enjoying that lends brilliance to life.

About Enjoyment—in One's Self, by One's Self, and for One's Self

In trying to analyze our fourth psychosocial resource we are not likely to find ourselves talking of anything more unexpected than grief; but analysis brings out some oddities with respect to the self-system, too. If you remember the discussion of the parent-determined images of good-me and bad-me, you will recall that the small child is motivated to engage with stress because the feelings associated with bad-me are so very unpleasant that the child moves almost pseudopodially to escape them, turning now in this direction, now in that, until he chances on a movement that lessens his discomfort and lets some of the recognizable good feelings flow back into him. It is an interpersonal process insofar as both the unpleasant and the pleasant feelings are parent-generated, but it is marked by an intrapersonal awareness of the difference between good feelings and bad; and this is a significant extension of the child's experience. We noted earlier that for the small child who is just beginning to approach cognitive thinking there is no way of evaluating "good" except by contrast with "bad," and this is the learning component of his awareness; but there is another part that has to do simply with awareness itself.

Awareness is broader and deeper when it encompasses bad feelings as well as good, and the novel and strange as well as the familiar and comforting. Thus in a sense we *enjoy* bad feelings because (a) they widen the range of our experience, and (b) they enhance good feelings by supplying contrast. A revision of Platt's design may illustrate. Suppose we draw two circles, mirror images of each other, but drawn with broken lines to suggest that they represent potential, on the one hand for "good," on the other hand for "bad," and then superimpose upon them a third circle drawn in a solid line to represent the real self, like this:

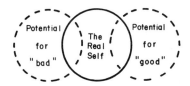

The design is a gross oversimplification of "the real self," but it suggests plainly enough that we do incorporate in our real selves some actualization of our potential for "good" and some actualization of our potential for "bad," and they do not have to be incorporated in equal amounts to give us a satisfying sense of psychological balance. We gain that satisfaction simply from becoming aware that we have actualized and enclosed within our real selves some part of both kinds of potential. Awareness lends immediacy that we relish for its own sake. At the same time it affords us that privy self-knowledge that adds to our self-esteem by letting us say, So this and that cheap and dirty thing I did do, but all of those other cheap and dirty things that I might have done, I didn't do. If we deny or ignore or fail to recognize in full our potential for wrongdoing, we have nothing with which to counterbalance all that portion of our "good" potential that we have failed to actualize.

All of our fantasy life is implicated here, too, in both its negative and its positive aspects. With respect to the negatives, our daydreams can serve as a safety valve for our hostilities, permitting us to do in fantasy what conscience or reason would never permit us to do in actuality. Many of us, who by and large have little anger or carry it lightly, could produce Rorschach protocols that would be judged seriously pathological by anyone not present during the testing process. The protocol by itself would not discriminate between unconscious and therefore dangerous hostility, and hostility that has been recognized and is deliberately dealt with through fantasy. That it is fantasy takes away nothing from the satisfaction that it offers, but spares us all the regrets and remorse that would overwhelm us if we acted out our hostilities, and the guilt that would burden us if we repressed them altogether. Similar benefits come in psychotherapy when the patient is encouraged to verbalize his hostile feelings. The difference is that such verbalizations usually erupt from a disturbed person in fierce urgency, whereas in healthy people they may often come out in the spirit of play.

There is little need to dwell in any detail on the positive enjoyments that daydreaming offers. Fantasied fulfillment of deeply cherished wishes may not add as much to our happiness as actual fulfillment would, but often can be more many-splendored than the real thing, and in any case is a lot better than nothing at all. Few of us would be candid enough to acknowledge publicly how countless are the wonderful things we can think of that people might say about us or do for us if they just would. For your private amusement I recommend that you take note of those wonderful things from time to time; and you need not feel embarrassed, because what we are really doing in this lovely occupation is elaborating one or another part of our ego ideals, defining for ourselves more and more specifically the kind of person we want to be. I merely add that it can be gloriously funny to catch oneself in the process.

Of course, to get this extra charge out of one's fantasy life requires the help of one's Observer, plus the capacity to enjoy him. Only if we are not too self-engulfed or self-encompassed can we enjoy the gaping discrepancy between our longings and aspirations, on the one hand, and our Observer's cool and discerning appraisal, on the other. This is the heart of any deep-reaching sense of humor, which is not concerned to reduce anxiety, but is ready and willing to embrace ambiguity. Let me try to bring this clear. Laughter, as Bower puts it, is triggered off by the sudden splitting apart of the cognitive and affective modes of perceiving. We get two diametrically opposite kinds of messages at the same time, one from the heart and one from the head, and this confronts us with ambiguity. If we are already inse-cure, such a discrepancy is alarming—there is nothing funny about it at all. But if, to begin with, we are fairly secure, then we can enjoy the ambiguity as the unexpected and therefore the entertaining.

For example, we have here and there in our offices copies of a list of six statements under the heading of *Murphy's Laws* (18). Each statement begins in a soberly reasonable or unctuously trite way, stimulating one to earnest attentiveness, a set to learn: and then each statement is rounded out in one or another unexpected way, sometimes unctuously, sometimes flatly, but always with the result that cognitive understanding is suddenly split off from the affective set. Here they are (and I have taken the liberty of inserting dashes to separate the one kind of message from the other):

1. In any field of scientific endeavor, anything that—can go wrong will go wrong.
2. Left to themselves, things always—go from bad to worse.
3. If there is a possibility of several things going wrong, the one that will go wrong is—the one that will do the most damage.
4. Nature always—sides with the hidden flaw.
5. Mother Nature—is a bitch.
6. If everything seems to be going well, you—have obviously over-looked something.

One way of defending ourselves against disappointment is to expect the worst, and *Murphy's Laws* can be viewed as that kind of defense; but it seems to me to come through clearly that whoever wrote it had been frus-trated and perhaps began to write it savagely, but then went on to elaborate the series with real enjoyment. It sounds more like the work of someone's Observer than like a defense.

Humor of this kind, embracing ambiguity and enabling us to laugh at ourselves in the predicaments that we get ourselves into, is one of the stur-dier parts of enjoyment because it is also able to serve us defensively. It does not succumb to the disapproval of others anything like so easily as our more defenseless enjoyments do. But the capacity for humor is like the capacity to enjoy in that it can be submerged for years at a stretch, and then—given the right conditions—surge up again into liberating laughter. It is necessarily submerged whenever ambiguity becomes too threatening, as it often does in adolescence. We find many small children who can laugh heartily at themselves, as Jennifer does when we surprise her by saying "I didn't mean to" before she can say it; but we find very few adolescents who are able to laugh at themselves—they are too engrossed in trying to establish the specifically-me, which by definition wants to be clean of ambiguities, leaving ambiguity looking like the archenemy. The adolescent's most urgent and often nearly desperate need is to be sure about himself, to know exactly who and what he is.

But it would be grossly misleading to suggest that no adolescent can laugh at himself, or that every adult can, and it would be overlooking a very important variable if we were simply to say that humor goes out with our sense of security. A large and lively sense of curiosity can outstrip the need for security, and the claims of our vanity as well. For pure self-enjoyment, of course, nothing quite equals the actualization of some part of our ego ideals, unless it is discovering from someone else some positive part of the specifically-me that we had not been conscious of before. Yet most of us remain oblivious to how much we could add to others' self-enjoyment by verbalizing the positive specifics that we see in them, by saying to the small child, "Johnny, you always wear such a bright *Good-morning* face that it's a pleasure to see you come in," or to the adult colleague, "I wonder if you know, if you fully appreciate, how eloquent your hands are."

Nevertheless, we all elicit negative reactions from others from time to time, and some of these can be piercingly hurtful, as when you reach out in friendship to some new acquaintance and are rebuffed. But here is where the lively curiosity comes into play. As you begin to puzzle out why the rebuff, what part of it is due to something within the other person, and what part to something heretofore unrecognized in yourself, you are likely to learn something more about yourself, and—let us face it—nothing is more interesting to most of us than this, no matter what the "something more" may be. People may go into psychoanalysis because they are in trouble, but they stay in analysis only if they become caught up in the fascination of learning more about themselves.

Perhaps one of the unformulated prayers of healthy people is "Give us this day our daily due of self-clarification." We tend to leave it unformulated because at first thought it sounds like sheer narcissism; but if you take second thought, you realize that the narcissistic person is not the least bit interested in self-clarification, but only in self-glorification. Such a person would always swerve from learning anything about himself that might detract from his "image." The curious person is so intent on his search for meaning that he will look anywhere and at anything in the hope of finding it. Understanding himself is far more important to him than admiring himself, and is far more satisfying, too. We enjoy understanding, and we enjoy it the more as we understand better.

This is fortunate because, since we have to learn somewhere in the course of our lives to become a good parent to ourselves, we need enough self-understanding to let us relax into self-acceptance. When we discussed this matter earlier, it was chiefly in terms of the foresight and guidance and discipline necessary to the attainment and maintenance of a life pattern with optimal balance and freedom of choice. The emphasis was on safeguarding against the sense of worthlessness or the feelings of emptiness that too often mar our later years, rather than on the fact that good parents also make sure that their children have ample opportunity for enjoyment. This is not always easy. People (parents, grandparents, aunts and uncles, and older siblings) who go through many years of requiring themselves to be dependable for the children who are dependent upon them, and denying themselves opportunities for enjoyment in order to create more such opportunities for the children, often become stuck in the pattern of dependability and self-denial, and continue in it long after it has become unnecessary and inappropriate. Being altruistic offers its own particular kind of enjoyment, but it need not and should not preclude our being occasionally self-indulgent, giving a present to ourselves without feeling guilty about it.

A word of warning here again: Young people accustomed to being the beneficiaries of our altruism may react quite negatively to having that source of supplies cut off or even cut down. It is a part of wisdom, therefore, to plan a gradual shifting over the years, from mainly giving to others while giving little to ourselves, to giving mainly to ourselves and only occasionally to others. In addition to planning, there is advantage in announcing the plan well before starting to carry it out. My grandmother, who lived her first fifty years in poverty, would tell us periodically, "I'm going to get more selfish as I grow older. I'm going to have more cream and sugar in my coffee, and more honey on my toast." My mother, at forty, began to say, "I'm going to grow more extravagant about my clothes as I grow older. I intend to substitute style for youth, and I'll expect you all to admire my stylishness." And we had so much enjoyment in Grandmother's enjoyment when she poured out her sweets with a lavish hand, we have so much enjoyment in my mother's enjoyment in her always stylish dress, that I am convinced that this is a way of sharing enjoyments, regardless of who may be their first recipient.

I should be embarrassed to say such things in these times of increasing recognition of the widespread and abysmal poverty in this country, unless I said at the same time that I think the most devastating effect of poverty is the stricture that it places on enjoyment. If we gave everyone in the country enough to live on and have some enjoyment in living, we should have a more affluent rather than a less affluent society than we have now when we are squandering so much of our wealth to deal with the consequences of poverty, while perpetuating the poverty itself. Until we eliminate poverty, every mental health professional of conscience will be hung up on the fact that our work is totally irrelevant to people who lack the bare necessities of life. But note this: Given just a fraction more than it takes to cover the necessities of life, it is possible to be extravagant. The word means only "exceeding the limits of reason or necessity." To be even just a little extravagant is a liberating experience of astonishing proportions, probably inversely related to the amount of money involved. I doubt that any millionaire could get as much enjoyment out of buying a second yacht or a third Cadillac as my grandmother got from the extra spoonful of honey on her toast.

For all of us who are neither impoverished nor wealthy, being extravagant may mean buying something that we want but don't have to have, or may mean such simple things as being no longer tightly scheduled to the clock, not always reachable by telephone, not feeling compelled at all times to do one's best, or even, as we grow old, in no longer feeling that the future stretches endlessly ahead of us, fraught with innumerable, unforeseeable contingencies that we had better provide against. That may sound like cold comfort, but since our futures do grow shorter as our pasts grow longer, and our pasts gradually include in reality a number of those unforeseeable contingencies, eventually we reach the point of recognizing that the time has come to be as freely extravagant and to follow our own inclinations as far as our resources allow. Being a good parent to oneself at this juncture means becoming a somewhat more indulgent parent, with a happier, more enjoying child.

Optimally it also includes the tranquillity of accepting oneself for what one is, faults and foibles, deficits, demerits, and all, and feeling no longer any compelling need to change Neither self-admiration nor self-fulfillment is essential to this kind of self-acceptance; and it has nothing to do with virtuousness. It is not so much positive as it is simply peaceful and conflict-free. There are plenty of pathological ways of being conflict-free, but for all of us who have had to struggle toward the attainment of integrity, any time of feeling conflict-free is an enjoyment of high order.

About Enjoyment—in Relation to One's Work and One's World

When Quentin Rae-Grant asked me, a few years ago, where creativity came into this formulation of mental health, I replied off the top of my head, "In enjoyment." I think the reply was essentially accurate, but it tells us little. I am not an expert on creativity, I am not even fully conversant with our literature on the subject, but if you will bear with my groping again, I should like to discuss it here, first because it is the conspicuous peak in the range of work, and second because I should like to dispel some of the mystique that still obscures its origins and *inhibits its growth*. As long as we think of it as a special gift that Nature bestows upon some people and withholds from others, there is obviously nothing that we can do about it. But if we discover through longitudinal studies that a large population of creative small children dwindles to a small population of creative adults, then obviously there is something that we can do about it.

It will be more productive, and may well be more accurate, too, if we conceive of creativity as we earlier conceived of IQ, that is, as in larger part the result of the *interaction* between what we are born with and the shaping influences of our life experience. We would assume, then, that creativity is a part of every healthy baby's potential, and that certain kinds of life experience allow the potential to develop freely, while other kinds stultify and even stifle its growth. To determine what the critical differences are between these two kinds of life experience will be a major undertaking; but a necessary first step will be to try to define a little more exactly what it is that we mean by the term "creativity."

We can do no more than make a beginning on this, but let us start where Freud left off, with the statement that "imaginative creation, like daydreaming, is a continuation of and substitute for the play of childhood" (4). This is almost an explicit statement that creative people are distinctly more childlike than uncreative people, particularly in the tenacity with which they hold onto the spirit of play. We have already noted the baby's evident delight in his first vocalizings and in his becoming able to grasp what he reaches for and get it into his mouth, literally in his every new accomplishment in learning to use his own body to do what he wants to do; and this is the same delight that we see in children as they acquire new play-skills, and the same delight that we see in the fledgling artist (14) or the master artist as he begins to give external shape and form to what earlier had been only a compelling drive within him. The real pay-off of hard work is the acquisition of skills so surely adroit that we can play with them: there is no headier elation than that which fills us when we play with such skills and suddenly realize that we're performing "clear over our heads," as we put it. Look at the face of the next great musician you hear, who wins a standing ovation. Look at the faces of the entire troupe taking curtain calls after a show of surpassing brilliance. You'll see the glow, precisely the same kind of lighting up that you see in the baby or the young child with a brand-new, astonishing achievement.

But creative people are also more childlike, I think, in their almost limitless capacity to be delighted by almost innumerable things and in a remarkably unfading way. That "remarkably unfading way" suggests an unusual immediacy, and since delights do not often move toward people, this must mean that these people move toward their delights—and immerse themselves in them. And when you begin to look at their delights, you find that they derive not just from the spirit of play, but also from the sense of wonder. Babies and small children and creative people are fascinated with what is in the world around them. The rapt look of wonder on a baby's face when someone holds him and, cheek to cheek, whispers softly in his ear is replicated over and over again as we hand down from one generation to the next our own fun-kinds of learning. Everyone who knows well how to play with small children is just as susceptible as the small child is to the magic of seeing a dancing sunspot on the wall as one tilts a hand mirror this way and that, or—better still—by the flight and pursuit of two such sunspots, as two people play the game; or of seeing the transformation of two human hands into the shadow of a duck's head or a donkey's head on the wall; of watching a thin flat soapy film expand into a shimmering sphere of streaming iridescence, and then vanish, leaving nothing of itself except a bit of soapy spatter; or of looking at one's world through a prism, or of seeing a flower, a leaf, a tiny seashell under a magnifying glass; of folding paper and snipping with a scissors here and there to produce a yard-long array of dancing dolls, or of working a loop of string on one's fingers into intricate patterns that can be undone in a trice, but in one way only.

From the psychological point of view, then, the differences between a Shakespeare and a Shaw, a Cole Porter and a Beethoven, a Van Gogh and a Walt Kelly, are almost incidental to the quality that they have in common —the manifest evidence in their work of their capacity to be completely enthralled with what they were doing and with the world in which they were doing it. But I had a patient once, in a state hospital, who had the same capacity. He was nineteen years old, mentally retarded, and labeled schizoid; but we found a job for him in a firm that made artificial flies for fishermen, and he became fascinated with tying the brightly colored flies, hour after hour and day after day. By virtue of his untiring enjoyment in working at his play or playing at his work (whichever way you choose to put it), there was less difference between him and a Lalique than between him and a bored postal clerk who sorts mail day after day and has forgotten how to find delight in anything. I would call the boy creative, as I would call anyone creative who finds joy in being productive, regardless of the quality of the product. I am quite willing to call it low-level creativity, but that boy had in full measure the three essential ingredients—the spirit of play, the sense of wonder, and the full investment of himself in what he was doing.

If in fact these are the three essential ingredients of creativity, then logic suggests that high-level creativity simply requires their further elaboration and ultimate integration, resulting in the delivery of beauty in a "spire of meaning" (5). I am not proposing to attempt a thoroughgoing analysis of the process, which seems to me exceedingly complex; but I should like to discuss the elaborations far enough to make clear the one condition that is indispensable to them all. Getzels and Jackson, analyzing differences between high-IQ students and high-creativity students, found that the most salient distinction between them was that the high-creativity students were characterized by a quick sense of humor, which was notably lacking in the high-IQ students (6). By "a quick sense of humor" they mean the ability to play with ideas in surprising and amusing ways, so that the finding reaffirms the importance of the spirit of play. But their study suggests (at least as I interpret it) a significant extension of the spirit of play, in the following way.

The high-creativity students were also competent in achievement, and to the same degree as the high-IQ students. The critical difference between them lay in the way in which they dealt with their competence. Both necessarily had developed their relevant skills via many of the not-fun kinds of learning; but in the process the high-IQ students really abjured all play in favor of furthering their achievement, and thus they became encased in what Wiener calls "the mental strait jacket which regulates the pattern of behavior" (25). The high-creativity students, on the other hand, began to play with their skills as soon as they had acquired them, elaborating and further refining them through play, and thus keeping themselves free of mental strait jackets, free to explore and to experiment and to become original.

It is relatively unimportant that only a few of these free people will produce something totally new and truly unique. Most high-creativity people build on the work that others have done before them, with the result that it can happen and has happened that two people, half a world apart and having no knowledge of what each other is doing, make the same discovery or devise the same new technique or invent essentially the same new tool at almost exactly the same point in time. It subtracts nothing from the achievement that it turns out to be not "unique." Both people started from the same base of what was already general knowledge, and then worked equally hard to find and put into the service of their intention whatever basic principles best fitted the need, and came up with the same answer. The larger part of what we call high creativity is simply the result of someone's putting intensive effort into doing something that had not been done before in quite the same way.

This is the larger part of it, quantitatively speaking, because it involves on the one hand the extension of the spirit of play into exploration and experimentation and originality, and on the other hand the extension of the full investment of self into the hard work that yields proficiency in all the necessary relevant and some apparently irrelevant skills. But qualitatively speaking, the key part of high creativity is still lacking until the sense of wonder is extended into the search for meaning and that search becomes so intensively compelling that it draws the other two extensions into the service of its single-minded pursuit.

Notice, now, the one condition that is indispensable for any—for all—of these extensions: namely, freedom to grow. Einstein put the point bluntly, saying: "It is, in fact, nothing short of a miracle that the modern methods of instruction have not yet entirely strangled the holy curiosity of inquiry; for this delicate little plant, aside from stimulation, stands mainly in need of freedom; without this it goes to wreck and ruin without fail" (3). A part of the wealth of the unrealized potential in all of us is, I suggest, a wealth of undeveloped creativity that might have been developed *if* our significant Others had recognized it in our childhood years and allowed us freedom enough to develop it. For many of us such recognition and allowance of freedom can still be of benefit, even though we reached adulthood without having had it; and for all of us the least we can do in common decency is to accord children freedom enough to decide for themselves the kind of work they most want to do.

But this freedom that others can grant us, the freedom from overrestrictive controls from outside of us, is only part of the freedom that we need if we are to grow. Einstein's "holy curiosity of inquiry" is an active thing; so is the spirit of play, so is the full investment of oneself, and so, preeminently, is the search for meaning. To develop and maintain all of these active thrusts demands that we learn somehow to keep free of the mental strait jackets that our anxieties and ambivalences and unresolved conflicts are always ready to strap us into. We have to ask here, Is this realistically possible? If there are, as we have been saying all along, ups and downs in the amount of energy available to us for dealing effectively with such stressors as anxiety, ambivalence, and unresolved conflicts, can we reasonably hope to keep always free of mental strait jackets? And doesn't the available-energy construct adequately account for the fact that not even the most productive person can be productive all of the time?

Again I have to go roundabout in trying to respond to these questions. Let us begin with a study done by John Clausen, in what might be called the process of psychiatric breakdowns (2). His central finding was that the earliest signs of impending disorganization in his patients had occurred in their closest relationships, particularly in the conjugal relationships, and that they clung to their work-responsibilities, however poorly they fulfilled them, often up to the very day of their hospitalizations. That finding stimulates speculation along several different lines, all relating enjoyment to work and work-responsibilities.

First, it is probably beyond dispute, demonstrated repeatedly in everyone's experience, that enjoyment is the first of our four psychosocial resources to succumb to unmanageable stress. One would expect that in disappearing it would reverse the course it followed (according to our theory) in appearing: that is, first dropping out of one's work, where it developed last and with most difficulty, then dissolving out of the self-system, and finally finding its last refuge where it began, in our most significant interpersonal relationships. I suggest that this *is* what happens in healthy people. One would also expect, however, that enjoyment would disappear first from wherever it is least entrenched; and Clausen's finding may therefore mean that the critical difference between growth toward mental health and increasing vulnerability to mental illness lies in the strength or the weakness of the interpersonal network.

A second line of speculation relates to what it was that kept those patients working even after they could no longer work very well. There was no implication that they were enjoying whatever activities they carried out in their work; and there was no implication that they conceptualized their work as "earning their own keep" or "pulling their own fair share of the weight." We are left to infer that they found a kind of security in their work that they found nowhere else: it was something that they could remain attached to, a familiar that was still familiar after everything else had become alien. It seems clear that there is a positive in the very fact of having committed oneself to something. For the sick person that positive may be no more than a comforting touch of security, enjoyable only in the respect that it is comforting when everything else is discomforting. But if responsibility and commitment hold a weak positive for sick people, they should hold a strong positive for healthy people; and as we begin to conjecture what that positive is, we can return to our earlier question about how we can keep free of mental strait jackets.

The available-energy construct is still generally applicable. It is totally applicable in the extreme situations. Vigorous people with ample energy delight in coping; and utterly depleted people cannot cope. But the great majority of us are in the middle ranges between these two extremes: we know times when we are tired and hard beset without being totally depleted, and we know other times when we have a fairly good supply of energy, but honestly question whether what we might gain by coping would be worth the expenditure of effort that it would cost. In all of these situations the easier out, assuming that we are not already in some mental strait jacket that compels us always to cope or always to avoid coping, is to let the matter ride, to do nothing. But this is no way to ensure our continuing freedom. To ensure our freedom we have to exercise our freedom, which means that we must choose between alternatives whenever choice offers.

We might call this the active stance, or we might call it the habit of courage, and I am choosing here to call it the latter, although you have to hunt hard to find the term in our professional literature. We have been so absorbed in studying "coping behavior" that we have almost overlooked the fact that whenever we feel anxious or ambivalent or irresolute, courage is the essential antecedent of effective coping behavior. And by bringing our anxieties and our responsibilities together with "a degree of atomic intimacy and precise orientation" (27) that transmutes them into effective coping, courage may well be the catalyst of our capacity for enjoyment. It requires some expenditure of energy, of course, to "summon up our courage," as we commonly put it, but for every modicum of energy thus invested, there is an astonishingly large yield of freedom.

In our earlier discussion of responsibility, I suggested that it brought us the double reward of strengthening our significant interpersonal relationships and of lending us the serenity that comes from having ordered our priorities and made our commitments. Certainly such rewards carry enjoyment; but again I think we shortchange ourselves if we remain unaware of the part that quiet courage plays in dispensing with bargaining, in committing ourselves to responsibility, and then in carrying out our commitments. To know that one has one's share of courage, to know what it feels like to call it into service and find it ample to our need—this is a liberating experience, and a deep enjoyment, too.

A Beginning of Further Exploration

Our concept of enjoyment as a psychosocial resource has—shall we say?—grown up in the course of the past five or six years. This is not due to our research, which deals only with the childhood of the concept, and with little if any forevision of how it would mature. Its maturation is due in large part to what happens in the intensive teacher workshops that I mentioned earlier, specifically to what happens in the Enjoyments sessions that come near the end of the ten-day period.

It is necessary, first, to summarize briefly the design of the workshops and the group process leading up to these sessions (and from one group to another there are only minor variations in that process) (24). Most of the participants have chosen to attend the workshop, so that they come well motivated to learn. Some of them will know two or three others in the group, some will have had no previous acquaintance with anyone else; all of them come from their homes in the morning, and return to their homes in the late afternoon. Nevertheless, they become a group-group very quickly, partly no doubt out of simply knowing that they will be together for seven hours a day, five days a week for two weeks, but partly also, I think, because I am an import, an unknown quantity, and they need to feel strong enough collectively to defend themselves against me, should I prove to be attacking. They move instinctively into the classroom pattern; and while they do not verbalize it, their insistence on my accepting the teacher role is almost palpable. Without verbalization we compromise on this: I assume responsibility for launching the workshop, but conduct it like an open seminar, inviting discussion or challenge at any point, but not requiring anything of them, leaving them free to choose their "critical distance" (16) and to modify that only when and as they please.

We go through the earlier material much as it is presented here in the preceding chapters, beginning with a predominantly intellectual approach that makes only casual reference to feelings. The group listens attentively, takes notes, from time to time raises a question about some point that hasn't been made quite clear; but there is little or no active discussion—the group is still uncertain about me. It is not until we begin to consider inter-personal relationships and dependency needs that they really accept me into the group, a development signalized by their chilly politeness toward any outsider who enters the room for whatever good reason, and by their almost visibly drawing closer to each other and to me when the intruder retreats and the door closes behind him.

It should be no cause for surprise that this material evokes deep feeling, to the point of tears in some people in every group. Any time you ask peo-ple to become more helpfully sensitive to children's feelings, you are inevi-tably asking them to become more aware of their own feelings, both past and present, and this is an intensely personal and often painful experience. The almost total silence that prevails at the end of the discussion of inter-personal relationships is a pregnant and hurting silence. No one has any comment to make, and they go their separate ways homeward; but from comments they make later, it is clear that most of them go home to go over the material in minute detail with whoever is closest to them, husband or wife, parents or friends. They don't really know quite what to do, I think, with so much feeling, and so, although the material on the self-system is easier, and most of the group become active participants in that discussion, anxiety continues to mount in them through the first week. They are quite conscious of this, some of them making no bones about the fact that they long for the weekend and the relief that it will bring from the workshop stress.

When they reassemble on the second Monday, their anxiety level is obviously lower; but if I mention this, I am likely to be shouted down with assurances that it will take just about half an hour or so to send it shooting up again. And it does mount again, although not to the earlier levels, because by this time their sense of security is also increasing. They can move energetically and with evident sureness into consideration of develop-ing competence, productivity, and responsibility; they are at home on their own ground here, and they argue issues back and fourth, vigorously but good-humoredly. Their introspection and their remembering have begun to pay off in a clearer sense of identity; their enforced close association with each other in the workshop hours has produced a feeling of "Well, so we're in the soup, but at least we're all in it together"; and they have become curious to a degree where their curiosity itself is stressful. Sometimes I wonder if they don't sense that they are moving as a group toward what Maslow calls "a peak experience" (17).

However that may be, I have learned from experience not to challenge such groups without forewarning, and so at the end of the discussion of

work as a psychosocial resource I give them their only homework assignment, asking them to come prepared to share with the group the next
morning any three experiences that have given them a moment of pure
enjoyment. Notice that I have given them none of the material presented
earlier in this chapter. In fact, when I have prefaced the homework assignment, as I sometimes have, by asking if anyone remembers what the fourth
postulated psychosocial resource was, no one remembers, and there is a
general scramble to look through their notes until I intervene and remind
them. Thus they approach the assignment without any guideline except the
proposition that enjoyment is a psychosocial resource, and they take it
almost elatedly, and a little jealously; as nearly as I can tell, no one wants
to talk with any other group member about the assignment. Instead, they
simply hurry home.

It is impossible to convey completely and exactly what goes on in the
Enjoyments sessions, but it is certainly not a lighthearted offering of commonplace superficialities. There is something oddly subdued and yet
momentous even about the way the group assembles the next morning.
There is less preliminary talk, and more thoughtful looking at each other,
followed by fleeting smiles when eyes meet eyes, and then looking away
again. As soon as I take my place at the lectern, the room becomes silent.

Then the group peak experience begins. The first contributions naturally come from among the freer, more outgoing members of the group, but
they are unmistakably sharing on the level of personal intimacy, quietly
and openly at first, and then hedging just a little in case they may be going
further than the group wants to go. Let me quote as nearly verbatim as I
can the beginnings of two recent sessions, so that you can see how like they
are. The initiators in both cases were women. The first said: "I guess being
alone on the seashore is one of the great times for me. I adore my family,
and I love to see them playing in the surf, but when Daddy takes all the
children on an expedition, and I can go down to the beach alone—that's
always a very special time. . . . And then I remember a party we went to,
and getting all involved with a lot of people and a lot of noisy talk, and
suddenly looking up and meeting my husband's eyes clear across the
room—nothing more than that, just the glance that sort of said, 'Hi, sweet-
ie!' . . . And then I guess my third enjoyment came from a boy I was
tutoring last year, who couldn't read and couldn't seem to relate to anybody, and then suddenly one day he was reading, and he looked at me in an
absolutely unbelieving way, and then he tried it again, and read some
more, and he looked at me again and smiled—the most beautiful smile!"
And the second woman, in a totally different group a year later: "Two

nights ago I had a long talk with my oldest child. It was the fullest communication we've ever had, and the way it deepened our relationship was something that I guess goes beyond words. . . . And then there was the day—my sister and I had been bitter rivals from the day she was born until that day, and it wasn't very many years ago, either—we became friends, and that was a red-letter day in my life. . . . And my third—I had a hyperactive child in my class last year, and I simply couldn't get through to him, and I don't know now what it was that I did or said that finally connected up with him, but I'll never forget the bright look on his face when he snapped to a salute and grinned and said, 'OK, chief!—got ya, chief!' "

Groups listen to beginnings like this with utmost attention and, I think, gratitude, because the responses follow so quickly and in kind. Soon everyone, including even the shyest and most reticent among them, is swept into the deep and incredibly strong current of feeling, and the term *enjoyment* seems to serve only as a sea anchor for anyone who may be fearful of going under momentarily, and who avoids a ducking by telling a joke. And so there are gales of laughter at times, as they tell of chagrins and embarrassments that only in retrospect could seem funny; but there are as many or more times of hushed, absorbed listening, and there are times when everyone is close to tears. Some speak shyly of things that they have done that made others happy, some describe gratefully things that others have done that made them feel loved. They talk of what most delights or touches them in their mates, their children, their parents, their students, their friends. Mothers talk of giving birth, fathers and uncles and aunts and grandmothers talk of the anxious waiting and then the joy of being told that a baby has been born. They speak of childhood experiences, and memorable moments in marriage, of watching someone growing old gracefully, or seeing someone's peaceful dying. Now and again someone pays a personal tribute to someone else in the group, setting off a round of applause. And not only does everyone contribute, but one round is never enough, because they touch off new associations in each other, sometimes a joke, oftener another remembered moving experience, a forgotten childlike pleasure, or a new perception. One very quiet, gentle woman, who seldom spoke, said suddenly and as if talking to herself, "There's a little spider crawling back and forth here on the floor by my chair, and I've been watching him, trying to figure out what he's trying to do, and—I'm *enjoying* a spider!"

The verbalized communications are a potpourri, but the underlying nonverbal communications seem singularly straightforward: for this space of time they throw aside their professionalism and all façades, and become just feeling human beings sharing their feelings and their loves with each other. Many of them might as well be saying, I've been blind, but now I'm seeing, and I've been deaf, but now I'm hearing, and I can taste and touch and smell and laugh and cry and talk and remember—and I can love and like and feel with all of us together. Others, though they couldn't go so far by themselves, and though they may in fact be shaken by the unexpected pull of so much feeling, go along and clearly want to go along. While the more timid ones take courage, the more aggressive ones are gentled; but everyone wants to give and to be given to. Within an hour everyone suddenly seems to feel so rich with experiential supplies that they have to be shared generously, even extravagantly. Over and over again there are references to something special that happened "last Friday night" or "last Saturday" or "last Sunday" when they had obviously used themselves more freely, more experimentally than they had in years, when they had discovered new meanings, and recognized feelings in themselves and others that they had not recognized before. Nobody seems to care whether they are moved to laughter or to tears; all that they seem to care about is that they are moved to deep feeling and that they feel enriched by it. They lend themselves unwithholdingly to the time and the place and the people, as we lend ourselves to our partners in dancing, in good conversation, in making love. They lend themselves to awareness of self and others, and to the human commitment and its risks, and with this they gain, at least for these few hours, the ease and the grace and the livingness of enjoying and being enjoyed.

All of this has been a totally unplanned and unforeseen development, and perhaps it has to be experienced to be believed. The group members themselves work very hard at trying to understand what is going on even while it is going on. They marvel first at how quickly and easily their defenses melt away, and occasionally someone will say, "We should have had this at the beginning, instead of so close to the end," but then most of the group will come out firm in their conviction that this couldn't have happened at the beginning, it could happen only after they had all sweated through so much together. (I might add here my own doubt that it could happen in a workshop using the same material but planned for fifteen weekly sessions of two hours each. Weekly sessions would not be likely to generate any feelings of "sweating it through together.")

Some groups marvel, also, at the kinds of things they talk about when they have been asked to talk about "enjoyments," questioning whether it is really possible for almost all of thirty people to arrive independently, overnight, and in the absence of guidelines, at the same position—the willingness to bring to the session some of their most cherished memories or most moving life experiences. But there was general agreement when one woman replied to this question, "Well, I can only speak for myself, but I just found I couldn't keep my mind on enjoyments. I kept remembering all of the things that have meant most to me, and so help me, I was in tears for the better part of two hours last night. The only belly-laugh I got out of it was when my husband asked what I was crying about, and I said, 'My enjoyments!' You should have seen his face! But then when I began to tell him some of the things I'd been remembering, he cried, too."

There can be little question, however, that the deep feeling expressed by one person elicits deep feeling in others, and that this is why the emotional surcharge steadily increases during the session, in spite of recurrent releases on waves of laughter. It was a man who put this most tellingly, a ruggedly masculine character who had just described as one of his "enjoyments" the birth of his second son just a year after his first son, still a baby, had died of nephritis. He had gone through the account very quietly except for clearing his throat a couple of times, and then paused; but when the young woman sitting next to him laid a gentle hand on his arm, he spread out his big hands and said, "Well, hell, when all your family is standing around there bawling for joy, you might as well bawl, too." He was defining his humanity.

This brings me to the one further thing that groups discover in this kind of voluntary sharing, and again I want to quote. Toward the end of one session a young woman, sensitive and searching but obviously very unsure of herself, exclaimed suddenly, "We've been freed!" To maintain a scientific stance I must add that not all participants feel so liberated, and that even for those who do, their liberation may be time-limited. But that girl was seeing accurately what was happening right then, that almost all in the group were coming out to be recognized for just the kind of human beings they really were, and coming out not only unafraid of being so recognized, but actively wanting to be.

Years ago, in my first attempt to formulate the power of enjoyment as a growth-promoting, energy-replenishing force, I suggested that it had this power by virtue of being both aim and end in one. It would be difficult to find a more comprehensive statement than that, or a more elusive one when you try to pin it down. But it takes substance now, I think, from the seeming paradox of the Enjoyments sessions. First, and from early childhood on, we lend ourselves unreservedly to whatever we enjoy; and then eventually we find enjoyment in thus lending ourselves, to whatever the moment and the moment's living call for. We grow most through those experiences (including grief) in which we immerse ourselves most completely; and we enjoy growing.

Chapter 6. A RESOURCE IS WHAT YOU HAVE BEFORE YOU NEED IT

The first time an Enjoyments session broke over me like an overwhelming wave and then rolled me up to ride its crest, when at last I could stop perseverating about it and begin to look ahead, I was besieged by misgivings about how the workshop would end. There was still one day left to go, and it was hard to see how it could be anything other than let-down and anticlimax after that amazing peak experience. Yet if that experience only opened doors that people then quickly closed again, to return to old patterns, it would mean less—and far less—than it had seemed to mean. The topic for the last day was already set, as it stands at the head of this chapter, and in my concern I spent the evening working out the obvious elaborations in the terms of our postulated mental health dimensions. They went about as follows.

First, since urgent need is more likely to impede than to promote the establishment of sound and enduring friendships, we shall be wise to develop a sustaining network of strong interpersonal relationships well in advance of a time of desperate need.

Second, we are all, throughout our lives, vulnerable to defeat, and for people whose sense of self includes the certainty of worth, defeat can be rock bottom on which to rebuild one's life; but for people who have never had any sure self-esteem, defeat is more likely to be a quagmire from which there is no rescue: therefore we shall do well to build, and in the process learn how to rebuild, our self-esteem before it is dealt a knockout blow.

Third, since it takes years of work to acquire those skills and attributes that eventually make us work-worthy, and opportunities and contingencies do not wait for years, we had better see to it that we have an age-appropriate amount of know-how, so that we can handle the contingencies when they occur and take advantage of the opportunities when they offer themselves.

Fourth, because chronic depression tends to move us in an ever-narrowing spiral involuting toward point, we should be alert to invite and embrace and continuously and ardently court the whatever-it-is that we have been calling "enjoyment," which moves us in an ever-expanding spiral out into the world around us.

I could have spared my efforts, and I should have been more trusting. That workshop group and others since then proved fully ready to address themselves to hard and sober work again on the next day. Given only the guideline that a resource is what you have before you need it, they themselves have taken over the discussion as their own appropriate task to work on. They talk about specific children, and they talk about classroom groups, always searching diligently for any strategies that might promote psychosocial growth. They accept the task as an ongoing one, in which they cannot expect closure in the sense of any neat and tidy rounding-off. They have at least a beginning appreciation of the difficulty inherent in any primary prevention effort, that of persuading people to work at developing a resource that they feel no immediate need to have. And they recognize that growth and mental health must always be open-ended, that the minute they become other than open-ended, they become something other than growth and mental health.

As a salute to their willingness to undertake so difficult a task, I am letting the title of this chapter stand as I put it to workshop groups. But a book must somehow be brought to an end, and this one should be brought to an open end: the only open end that I can see lies in the proposition that the psychosocial resources that we have been talking about are more than just what we have before we need them. They are also what we live on and live with and cannot sustain life and health and growth without. They are the psychological counterparts of the food and sleep and work and play that sustain our physical health and growth, but with a critical difference: food and clothing and shelter can be bought, even if with stolen money; and there is no way to buy or steal psychosocial resources. People who do not have them can do nothing except destroy and lay waste, or subside into the total inaction of despair.

We have only to look at the broader scene to gain some conception of how many millions of people are without the resources that would let them live decently. Our psychiatric facilities are crammed to capacity, and their waiting lists are long and growing longer. We have Glidewell's estimate of 3 million children (between the ages of five and twelve years!) in need of some special help, and 1.3 million of them who should be referred for psychiatric treatment if there were resources available to treat them (2). Our crime rates are high and surging higher. With every passing week it becomes more nearly impossible to recruit people to work in the inner cities—they are fearful, and with good reason, of the violence that prevails there, the robberies, the beatings, the rapes, the senseless murders. But in the suburbs as well as in the cities more and more of our young people, empty of aims and aspirations, are turning for kicks to drugs and delinquencies; and the extent of the vandalism occurring almost everywhere is blatant evidence that we have somehow aroused and unleashed a fury of hatred, of unprecedented scope and intensity.

If the laws of cause and effect apply, as we think they do, to human behavior, then the tragic waste and the appalling devastation that we are living with today are the results either of things that we have been doing, or of things that we have been failing to do, or of some combination of the two. If we are to change the outcomes, we shall have to change their causes. The scientifically correct procedure would be: first, to obtain information enough to allow us to determine which disorders are endemic, and which are epidemic, and where, and what their correlates are; second, on the basis of that information to design experiments aimed at eliminating or at least alleviating what seem to be the pathogenic factors involved; third, to continuously and thoroughly evaluate the experimental situation to see in what ways and to what degree it differs, or begins to differ, from the pre-experimental situation; and finally to repeat this entire series of steps as often as necessary to achieve the values we are seeking.

Derisive laughter (with underlying dismay) is a realistic response to such a proposal. The need for action now is urgent; epidemiological studies take time; the scientifically correct procedure is impracticable here. It might have been a most valuable resource for us if we had had the foresight to develop it in advance of our need. Lacking it, we can only improvise; but let us make no mistake about the fact that in improvising we shall be experimenting, too. I said at the outset that everyone who works with or for or in behalf of people is dealing with many unknowns and is therefore experimenting, but that there was nothing unforgivable about this *provided* that we evaluate the results of our experiments and learn from our mistakes. Let me add now that *we cannot choose not to experiment.* We can choose only whether to go about it wittingly or unwittingly, and whether to learn from it or not to learn from it.

Let us make no mistake, either, about the size and the nature of the major obstacle that will stand in our way, if we choose to experiment wittingly and with intent to learn. That obstacle is not the enormity of social ills "out there" that confronts us; it is, rather, what happens to us as we become more and more highly institutionalized (1). Both in the field of education and in the field of mental health, as in every other institution that we have established, there are two separate camps—the value-seekers in one, and the information-seekers in the other. In the natural course of institutionalized events the people in these two camps will have no truck with each other. Practitioners (the value-seekers) will spend themselves in practice, and researchers (the information-seekers) will spend themselves in research. Educators will labor feverishly within their own citadel, and mental health personnel will labor feverishly within theirs, each in their own ways preparing to sally forth against the enemy "out there." It is the age-old farce that the human race has always found so convenient, so congenial, and so comforting: envision the threat as coming from elsewhere, and there is no need for us to see that we are captives in our own institutions, and prisoners to our own professions.

We would do better to look into any clear mirror, because it is there that, as Walt Kelly puts it, "We shall meet the enemy, and not only may he be ours, he may be us" (4). That statement has been quoted (and misquoted) so frequently that we can infer the recognition by many people that "he" is indeed "us"; but I submit that our pressing problem is how to make him also "ours," no longer alienated and misperceived, but recognized, accepted, and restored to *belonging to us*. It is not a problem beyond our capacity to solve, if we have the courage to look into the mirror and recognize ourselves-collectively there. The reflection will not be altogether beautiful, persuading us to instantaneous and unqualified acceptance, but it will not have the institutional look; it will have the human look, mystified and mystifying, and appealing both to our compassion and to our curiosity.

We can learn to accept ourselves-collectively if we will indulge our curiosity and our compassion at the same time, cutting across professional barriers in order to understand ourselves better, through continuing communication gradually discerning our differing limitations and hang-ups, and our differing knowledges and skills, so that we can see how we might begin to work together, combining our resources into concerted effort, and serving and supporting each other while we serve and support ourselves.

But it is only the actual working together that can restore ourselves-collectively to belonging to us. It is not likely that our institutions, as institutions, will help us here. Institutions, developed initially to strengthen our thrusts toward progress by collective action, quickly become the fastnesses of the fearful, and all but impregnable to change from without. They are not proof, however, against change from within (witness what is happening within the Roman Catholic Church today); and our hope rests with those people in institutions who are willing to come out quietly from time to time, without fanfare, to enter into "temporary social systems" for specific problem-solving purposes. There, as Glidewell has pointed out (3), we can together define our problems, establish our priorities, and formulate, initiate, and carry out appropriate experiments to induce change for the better.

Thus, the pertinent question is not, Do we know enough to induce change for the better? It is simply, Do we care enough to try to learn? and Do we know enough to care? We have not, so far, shown much sign that we know enough to care. Over eight years ago Leon Eisenberg said, "We must act now, for there may be no tomorrow," and he quoted Hillel asking, almost 2,000 years ago, "If not now, when?" (1) To questions and challenges like these, people have always given the glib reply that there have been crackpots crying doom since time began, just as there are ravens among us now, croaking daily that time is running out; but we are still here today, just as we were yesterday and the day before. So much is painfully true: take us by and large, we are basically the same as we were yesterday and the day before, or 2,000 or 4,000 or 14,000 years ago, when we lived in caves, going out to stalk our prey, ourselves stalked by fear, and then returning to the security of the cave again, perhaps to eat, perhaps to sleep, perhaps to paint on the wall with matchless beauty of line and color and conformation the same beasts that we loved and feared and preyed upon.

We have not changed ourselves very much; we have only changed our world. It took Magellan three long years to circumnavigate the globe; today men can orbit it in an hour and a half and shoot on to the moon. When men first began to fight men, they used their fists or whatever hand-weapons they could fashion or hurl; today we have stockpiled nuclear weapons enough to erase all life from the face of the earth. These commonplace statements of today represent the noteworthy achievements of our technological prowess, which remains unconcerned with ourselves-collectively and with the fact that we are also well on the way to polluting ourselves out of existence.

The issue is still, Do we care enough to learn, and do we know enough to care? The choice is ours to make, and whether we make it deliberately or by default, it will be made. But unless we make it deliberately and in time, and thereby safeguard our right to choose, we have no sure defense against foreclosure on everything else that we possess or hope for. Nothing except the active stance can keep the end open.

REFERENCES

Author's Note

For this author the code of scholarship, which calls for precise citations of sources, poses a number of embarrassments. It is not that I think sources unimportant; on the contrary, as much as any other curious and critical reader I want to know the sources from which an author draws support for statements made or for speculations ventured. And it is not that the more comfortable posture for me is that of student rather than scholar, inquisitive rather than authoritative; precise citations are also required of students.

It is, rather, an odd assortment of problems. For one thing, the mental health theory outlined in this book is based on the work of Freud and Sullivan and Selye to a degree that could hardly be overstated; but that fact is certainly not reflected in my references. They reflect more clearly my regard for memorable terms—Galsworthy's "spire of meaning," Lorenz's "critical distance," Maslow's "peak experience"; but the also memorable "work of mourning" is not referenced—you can find it both in Freud's paper, "Mourning and Melancholia," and in Abraham's paper, "Development of the Libido," and while Freud's paper was published first, Abraham's was written first and sent to Freud, who frankly acknowledged that he borrowed heavily from it, without specifying *what* he borrowed: so to whom should the credit go? The difficulty takes a slightly different form in a Glidewell reference: some years ago he began to talk about "socially inept" children, but you will not find that term in the reference cited for it, because there it has become "interpersonal ineptness."

Another kind of problem involves my erratic memory. When I *think* that the "four parts male to three parts female" formulation is Virginia

157

Woolf's, and that the phrase "involuting to point" comes from Amiel, but have not been able to find either statement again, then I have to question whether "a brilliance of grief" is really my own phrase, as I think, or was simply absorbed from some forgotten source.

But there are also sources that forget! Since I often worked from unpublished papers and unrecorded conversations and discussions, I wrote to many people to ask them to check on my accuracy and to supply any missing or updated references. Three responses I particularly cherish. Bower replied: "I must say the statements which you attribute to me sound like me, but I'd be swigged if I can remember when I said them. Pick out a convenient time and let it go at that." And Bettye Caldwell replied: "I appreciate your wanting to quote me—I absolutely love to be quoted—and I apologize that I can't tell you where it is that I said the elegant things you are giving me credit for having said." Fortunately, my memory served to fill in those two gaps. The Caldwell reference is included in my list; and Bower's comments about laughter and games were part of the discussion at a session of the American Orthopsychiatric Association on March 21, 1968 (I was recorder for that session, and took extensive notes). I *feel* sure that the definition of walking as "a progressive series of aborted falls" was offered by Dr. Winthrop Phelps in an address delivered in St. Louis some- what over twenty-five years ago, and Dr. Phelps "thinks it is a good defini- tion and thoroughly agrees with it" and "has a feeling" that he probably did say it, but "cannot prove it!"

Finally, there is the matter of omissions. Where it would be unfair not to identify by name some of the people whom I have quoted directly, with their permission, it would constitute a breach of confidentiality to identify in the same way others whom I have quoted as directly—and I am thinking here in particular of the people in my workshop groups, where there is clearly a trusting assumption of privileged communication. Other omissions are due to my deplorable tendency to free-associate to the work of others as I write, instead of making a systematic survey of the relevant literature; and I feel almost as apologetic about such omissions as I do about my inability to record here, with my thanks, the names of all the friends and colleagues who helped me out of many perplexities.

As a result of all these things, the full list of my sources looks preten- tiously long and is still incomplete. Regretfully and regrettably I must leave it incomplete; but its length will concern me less, and I hope will concern the reader less, when the citations are grouped under chapter numbers. If this should turn out to be nothing more than a substitution of one speciosity for another, let me simply say, with Ralph Rackstraw in Gilbert's *H.M.S.*

Pinafore, "I am but a living ganglion of irreconcilable antagonisms. I hope I make myself clear . . . ?"

Introduction and Chapter 1 (pages vii to 17)

1. Eiduson, Bernice T.; Eiduson, Samuel; and Geller, Edward. "Biochemistry, Genetics, and the Nature-Nurture Problem." *American Journal of Psychiatry* 119 (1962): 342–350.

2. Eiduson, Samuel; Geller, Edward; Yuwiler, Arthur; and Eiduson, Bernice T. *Biochemistry and Behavior.* New York: Van Nostrand Reinhold Company, 1964.

3. Glidewell, John C., and Swallow, Carolyn S. *The Prevalence of Maladjustment in Elementary Schools.* Report to the Joint Commission on Mental Health of Children. Chicago: The University of Chicago, July 1968.

4. Grinker, Roy R., Sr., and Robbins, Fred P. *Psychosomatic Case Book.* New York: McGraw-Hill Book Company, 1954.

5. Horrobin, David F. *The Communication Systems of the Body.* New York: Basic Books, Inc., 1964.

6. McKay, D. M. "Comparing the Brain with Machines." *The American Scientist* 42, no. 2 (April 1954): 265–266.

7. Selye, Hans. *The Stress of Life.* New York: McGraw-Hill Book Company, 1956.

8. Shuttleworth, Frank K. "The Physical and Mental Growth of Girls and Boys Age Six to Nineteen, in Relation to Age at Maximum Growth." *Monographs of the Society for Research in Child Development,* vol. 4, serial no. 22, no. 3. Washington, D.C.: National Research Council, 1939.

9. Stringer, Lorene A.; McMahon, Lee; and Glidewell, John C. *A Normative Study of Academic Progress in Elementary School Children.* Progress Report I. Clayton, Mo.: St. Louis County Health Department, June 1961.

10. Stringer, Lorene A. "Parent-Child Relations in the Early School Years." *Social Work* 9, no. 2 (April 1964).

11. ———, and Glidewell, John C. "Early Detection of Emotional Illnesses in School Children." Final Report. Clayton, Mo.: St. Louis County Health Department, April 1967.

12. Wooldridge, Dean E. *The Machinery of Life.* New York: McGraw-Hill Book Company, 1966.

Chapter 2 (pages 18 to 45)

1. Bateson, Gregory. In *Communication,* by Jurgen Ruesch and Gregory Bateson. New York: W. W. Norton & Company, Inc., 1951.

2. Erikson, Erik H. *Childhood and Society.* New York: W. W. Norton & Company, Inc., 1950.

3. Kagan, Jerome. "Christopher—The Many Faces of Response." *Psychology Today* 1, no. 8 (January 1968).

4. Meehl, P.E. "Schizotaxia, Schizotypy, and Schizophrenia." *American Psychologist* 17 (1962): 827–838.

5. Rado, Sandor. "Adaptational Psychodynamics: A Basic Science." In *Changing Concepts of Psychoanalytic Medicine,* edited by Sandor Rado and George E. Daniels. New York: Grune and Stratton, Inc. 1956.

6. Stringer, Lorene A., and Pittman, David J. "The Unmeasured Residual in Current Research on Parental Attitudes and Child Behavior." In *Parental Attitudes and Child Behavior,* edited by John C. Glidewell. Springfield, Ill.: Charles C. Thomas, Publisher, 1961.

7. Sullivan, Harry Stack. *The Interpersonal Theory of Psychiatry.* New York: W. W. Norton & Company, Inc., 1953.

Chapter 3 (pages 46 to 82)

1. Baer, Donald M., and Wolf, Montrose M. "The Reinforcement Contingency in Pre-School and Remedial Education." In *Early Education,* edited by Robert D. Hess and Roberta Meyer Bear. Chicago: Aldine Publishing Company, 1968.

2. Beck, Aaron T. *Depression: Clinical, Experimental, and Theoretical Aspects.* New York: Harper and Row, Publishers, Inc., 1967.

3. Caldwell, Bettye M. *"Infant Socialization and Subsequent Behavior."* A paper presented at the 1965 annual meeting of the American Public Health Association, Chicago.

4. Dorsey, John M. "The Use of the Psychoanalytic Principle in Child Guidance Work." In *Searchlights on Delinquency,* edited by Kurt R. Eissler. New York: International Universities Press, Inc., 1949.

5. Flint, Betty M. *The Security of Infants.* Toronto: University of Toronto Press, 1959.

6. Freud, Sigmund. "The Ego and the Id." In *Complete Psychological Works of Sigmund Freud,* Standard Edition, revised and edited by James Strachey, vol. 19. London: The Hogarth Press, 1961; New York: W. W. Norton & Company, Inc., 1962.

7. ———. *New Introductory Lectures on Psychoanalysis,* translated and edited by James Strachey. New York: W. W. Norton & Company, Inc. 1933.

8. Glidewell, John C.; Kantor, Mildred B.; Smith, Louis M.; and Stringer, Lorene A. "Social Structure and Socialization in the Elementary School Classroom." In *Review of Child Development Research,* vol. 2, edited by Lois Wladis Hoffman and Martin L. Hoffman. New York: Russell Sage Foundation, 1966.

9. ———, and Swallow, Carolyn S. *The Prevalence of Maladjustment in Elementary Schools.* Report to the Joint Commission on Mental Health of Children. Chicago: The University of Chicago, July 1968.

10. ————. *Choice Points: Essays on the Emotional Problems of Living with People.* Cambridge, Mass.: The M.I.T. Press, 1970.

11. Greenacre, Phyllis. *Trauma, Growth and Personality.* New York: W. W. Norton & Company, Inc., 1952.

12. Harlow, Harry F. "The Heterosexual Affectional System in Monkeys." *American Psychologist* 17, no. 1 (January 1962).

13. ————, and Harlow, Margaret. "Social Deprivation in Monkeys." *Scientific American* 207, no. 5 (November 1962).

14. Harris, Florence R.; Wolf, Montrose M.; and Baer, Donald M. "Effects of Adult Social Reinforcement on Child Behavior." In *The Young Child: Reviews of Research.* Washington, D.C.: National Association for the Education of Young Children, 1967.

15. Hofstatter, Lilli; Friedman, Ellen; and Hofstatter, Leopold. "Mirror Room Technique in Profound Mental Retardates." Mimeographed. St. Louis, Mo.: St. Louis State School and Hospital, and Department of Psychiatry of Washington University School of Medicine, 1964.

16. Langner, Thomas S., and Michael, Stanley T. *Life Stress and Mental Health.* Glencoe, Ill.: The Free Press, 1963.

17. Lavin, David E. *Prediction of Academic Performance: A Theoretical Analysis and Review of Research.* New York: Russell Sage Foundation, 1965.

18. Maslow, Abraham H., and Mittelmann, Bela. *Principles of Abnormal Psychology.* New York: Harper & Brothers, Publishers, 1941.

19. Miller, Arthur A.; Isaacs, Kenneth S.; and Haggard, Ernest A. "On the Nature of the Observing Function of the Ego." *British Journal of Medical Psychology* 38 (1965): 161–169.

20. Milne, A.A. "In the Dark." In *Now We Are Six.* New York: E.P. Dutton and Company, Inc., 1927; London: Methuen & Co., Ltd., 1927. (Quoted by permission, courtesy of C.R. Milne).

21. Piaget, Jean. *The Construction of Reality in the Child.* Translated by Margaret Cook. New York: Basic Books, Inc., Publishers, 1954.

22. Raush, Harold, and Sweet, Blanche. "The Preadolescent Ego: Some Observations of Normal Children." *Psychiatry* 24, no. 2 (May 1961): 122–132.

23. Redl, Fritz, and Wineman, David. *Children Who Hate.* Glencoe, Ill.: The Free Press, 1951.

24. Ribble, Margaret A. "Infantile Experience in Relation to Personality Development." In *Personality and the Behavior Disorders,* edited by J. McV. Hunt, vol. 2. New York: The Ronald Press Company, 1944.

25. Sarason, S.B.; Davison, K.S.; Lighthall, Fred F.; Waite, R.R.; and Ruebush, B.K. *Anxiety in Elementary School Children.* New York: John Wiley and Sons, Inc., 1960.

26. Short, James F., Jr. "Juvenile Delinquency: The Sociocultural Context." In *Review of Child Development Research,* vol. 2, edited by Lois Wladis Hoffman and Martin L. Hoffman, New York: Russell Sage Foundation, 1966.

27. Spitz, René. "Hospitalism: An Inquiry into the Genesis of Psychiatric Conditions in Early Childhood." In *The Psychoanalytic Study of the Child,* edited by Ruth S. Eissler et al., vol. 1, 53–74. New York: International Universities Press, 1945.

28. ———. "Anaclitic Depression." In *The Psychoanalytic Study of the Child,* edited by Ruth S. Eissler et al., vol. 2, 313–342. New York: International Universities Press, 1946.

29. Stringer, Lorene A., and Glidewell, John C. "Early Detection of Emotional Illnesses in School Children." Final Report. Clayton, Mo.: St. Louis County Health Department, April 1967.

30. Sullivan, Harry Stack. *The Interpersonal Theory of Psychiatry.* New York: W. W. Norton & Company, Inc., 1953.

31. ———. *Clinical Studies in Psychiatry.* New York: W. W. Norton & Company, Inc., 1956.

32. Taylor, Robert M. "Parental Reinforcement and the Adjustment of Sixth Grade Children." *American Journal of Public Health* 56, no. 9 (September 1966): 1512–1523.

33. Westley, William, and Epstein, Nathan B. *The Silent Majority.* San Francisco: Jossey-Bass, Inc., Publishers, 1969.

34. Wiener, Norbert. *The Human Use of Human Beings.* Boston: Houghton-Mifflin Company, 1954.

35. Woolf, Virginia. *The Common Reader.* New York: Harcourt Brace Jovanovich, Inc., 1925; London: Hogarth Press, Ltd., 1929. (Quoted by special permission, courtesy of Quentin Bell, Angelica Garnett, and the Hogarth Press.)

Chapter 4 (pages 83 to 116)

1. Caldwell, Bettye M. "What is the Optimal Learning Environment for the Young Child?" *American Journal of Orthopsychiatry* 37, no. 1 (January 1967.)

2. Davis, Robert B. *Discovery in Mathematics.* Reading, Mass.: Addison-Wesley Company, 1964.

3. Eble, Kenneth E. *A Perfect Education.* New York: The Macmillan Company, 1966.

4. Edwards, Allen L. *Experimental Design in Psychological Research.* New York: Holt, Rinehart & Winston, Inc., 1953.

5. Eiduson, Samuel; Geller, Edward; Yuwiler, Arthur; and Eiduson, Bernice T. *Biochemistry and Behavior.* New York: Van Nostrand Reinhold Company, 1964.

6. Garrett, Henry E. *Statistics in Psychology and Education.* 6th ed. New York: David McKay Company, 1966.

7. Haggard, Ernest A. "Socialization, Personality, and Academic Achievement in Gifted Children." *School Review* 65, no. 4 (Winter 1957): 388–414.

8. Hess, R.D., and Shipman, V.C. "Early Experience and Socialization of Cognitive Modes in Children." *Child Development* 36 (1965): 869–886.

9. Horn, John L. "Intelligence—Why It Grows, Why It Declines." *Trans-Action,* November 1967.

10. Jackson, Edith B. "Childbirth Patterns in the U.S." In *Mental Health and Child Development,* edited by Kenneth Soddy, vol. 1. New York: Basic Books, Inc. 1956.

11. Kagan, Jerome. "Christopher—The Many Faces of Response." *Psychology Today* 1, no. 8 (January 1968).

12. Levine, Murray. "Psychological Testing of Children." In *Child Development Research,* vol. 2, edited by Lois Wladis Hoffman and Martin L. Hoffman. New York: Russell Sage Foundation, 1966.

13. Livsey, C.D. "Soliloquy of a Drop-out." *The St. Louis Post Dispatch,* July 30, 1967.

14. Morse, Robert W. As quoted in a UPI Report, Cincinnati, February 25, 1967.

15. Moss, Howard, and Kagan, Jerome. "Stability of Achievement and Recognition Seeking Behaviours from Early Childhood through Adulthood." *Journal of Abnormal and Social Psychology* 62 (1961), no. 3:504–513.

16. Reichert, John J. "Competitive Athletics for Pre-teen-age Children." *Journal of the American Medical Association* 166, no. 14 (April 1958): 1701–1707.

17. Ribble, Margaret A. "Infantile Experience in Relation to Personality Development." In *Personality and the Behavior Disorders,* edited by J. McV. Hunt, vol. 2, 621–651. New York: The Ronald Press Company, 1944.

18. Riesen, Austin H. "Effects of Stimulus Deprivation on the Development and Atrophy of the Visual Sensory System." *American Journal of Orthopsychiatry* 30 (1960): 23–36.

19. ———. "Stimulation as a Requirement for Growth and Function in Behavioral Development." In *Functions of Varied Experience,* edited by Donald W. Fiske and Salvatore R. Maddi. Homewood, Ill.: The Dorsey Press, 1961.

20. ———. "Effects of Early Deprivation of Photic Stimulation." In *The Biosocial Basis of Mental Retardation,* edited by Sonia F. Osler and Robert E. Cooke. Baltimore: The Johns Hopkins Press, 1965.

21. Rosenthal, Robert, and Jacobson, Lenore. *Pygmalion in the Classroom: Teacher Expectation and Pupil's Intellectual Development.* New York: Holt, Rinehart, and Winston, Inc., 1968.

22. Sarason, S.B.; Davison, K.S.; Lighthall, Fred F.; Waite, R.R.; and Ruebush, B.K. *Anxiety in Elementary School Children.* New York: John Wiley and Sons, Inc., 1960.

23. Skeels, Harold M. "Adult Status of Children with Contrasting Early Life Experiences." *Monographs of the Society for Research in Child Development,* vol. 31, serial no. 105, no. 3. Chicago, 1966.

24. ———, and Skodak, Marie. "Techniques for a High-Yield Followup Study in the Field." *Public Health Reports* 80, no. 3 (March 1965): 249–257.

25. Sontag, L.W.; Baker, C.T.: and Nelson V.L. "Mental Growth and Personality Development: A Longitudinal Study." *Monographs of the Society for Research in Child Development,* vol. 13, serial no. 68, no. 2. Washington, D.C.: National Research Council, 1958.

26. Spitz, René. "Hospitalism: An Inquiry into the Genesis of Psychiatric Conditions in Early Childhood." In *The Psychoanalytic Study of the Child,* edited by Ruth S. Eissler et al., vol. 1, 53–74. New York: International Universities Press, 1945.

27. ———. "Anaclitic Depression." In *The Psychoanalytic Study of the Child,* edited by Ruth S. Eissler et al., vol. 2, 313–342. New York: International Universities Press, 1946.

28. Stennett, R.G. "Emotional Handicap in the Elementary Years: Phase or Disease?" *American Journal of Orthopsychiatry* 36 (1966):444–449.

29. Stringer, Lorene A. "Acceleration: Danger Sign?" In *Quarterly Journal of the Mental Health Association of St. Louis,* Spring 1959.

30. ———. "Report on a Retentions Program." *Elementary School Journal,* April 1960, 370–375.

31. ———. "Mental Health Consultation on School Policy." Paper read before a joint session of the Mental Health Section, School Health Section, and American School Health Association at the Meeting of the American Public Health Association, Chicago, October 1965.

32. Stringer, Lorene A., and Glidewell, John C. "Early Detection of Emotional Illnesses in School Children." Progress Report III. Clayton, Mo.: St. Louis County Health Department, August 1962.

33. ———. Ibid. Final Report. Clayton, Mo.: St. Louis County Health Department, April 1967.

34. White, Robert W. "Motivation Reconsidered: The Concept of Competence." *Psychology Review* 66 (1959):297–333.

35. Wiener, Norbert. *The Human Use of Human Beings.* Boston: Houghton-Mifflin Company, 1954.

Chapter 5 (pages 117 to 150)

1. Berne, Eric. *Games People Play.* New York: Grove Press, Inc., 1964; London: André Deutsch, Ltd., 1966.

2. Clausen, John A. "The Marital Relationship Antecedent to Hospitalization for Mental Illness." Mimeographed. Presented at a meeting of the American Sociological Association, Chicago, September 1959.

3. Einstein, Albert, as quoted by Jeremy Bernstein in "Books: Einstein and Bohr: A Debate." *The New Yorker,* April 16, 1966.

4. Freud, Sigmund. *Collected Papers,* edited by Ernest Jones, vol. 4. London: The Hogarth Press, 1949; New York: Basic Books, Inc., Publishers, 1959.

5. Galsworthy, John. "Some Platitudes Concerning Drama." *The Inn of Tranquility.* London: Heinemann, 1912; New York: Charles Scribner & Sons, 1926.

6. Getzels, Jacob W., and Jackson, Philip W. *Creativity and Intelligence.* New York: John Wiley and Sons, Inc., 1962.

7. Glidewell, John C.; Kantor, Mildred B.; Smith, Louis M.; and Stringer, Lorene A. "Social Structure and Socialization in the Elementary School Classroom." In *Review of Child Development Research,* vol. 2, edited by Lois Wladis Hoffman and Martin L. Hoffman. New York: Russell Sage Foundation, 1966.

8. Gold, Thomas. As quoted in *The St. Louis Post-Dispatch,* April 17, 1965.

9. Harlow, Harry F. "The Heterosexual Affectional System in Monkeys." *American Psychologist* 17, no. 1 (January 1962).

10. ———, and Harlow, Margaret. "Social Deprivation in Monkeys." *Scientific American* 207, no. 5 (November 1962).

11. ———. "Learning to Love." *Scientific American* 215, no. 3 (September 1966).

12. Hess, R.D., and Shipman, V.C. "Early Experience and the Socialization of Cognitive Modes in Children." *Child Development* 36 (1965):869–886.

13. Jahoda, Marie. "Mental Health." In *The Encyclopedia of Mental Health,* edited by Albert Deutsch and Helen Fishman, vol. 4. New York: Franklin Watts, Inc. 1963.

14. Kane, Henry. *How to Write a Song.* New York: The Macmillan Company, 1962.

15. Levine, Jacob. "Humor and Mental Health." In *The Encyclopedia of Mental Health,* edited by Albert Deutsch and Helen Fishman, vol. 3. New York: Franklin Watts, Inc., 1963.

16. Lorenz, Konrad. *Man Meets Dog.* Boston: Houghton-Mifflin Company, 1955.

17. Maslow, Abraham H. "Lessons From the Peak Experiences." In *Science and Human Affairs,* edited by Richard E. Farson, 45–54. Palo Alto, Calif.: Science and Behavior Books, Inc., 1965.

18. Murphy's Laws. Said to have been authored by leprechauns. Ferguson, Mo.: Jackson Supply Company, n.d.

19. Platt, John R. "Beauty: Pattern and Change." In *Functions of Varied Experience,* edited by Donald W. Fiske and Salvatore R. Maddi. Homewood, Ill.: The Dorsey Press, 1961.

20. Selye, Hans. *The Stress of Life.* New York: McGraw-Hill Book Company, 1956.

21. Stringer, Lorene A., and Glidewell, John C. "Early Detection of Emotional Illnesses in School Children." Final Report. Clayton, Mo.: St. Louis County Health Department, April 1967.

22. Stringer, Lorene A.; Glidewell, John C.; and Taylor, Robert M. "Mothers as Colleagues in School Mental Health Work." Proposal submitted to the National Institutes of Health, February 1965.

23. ———. "Research Interviews with Mothers as Entry into Primary Prevention." *American Journal of Public Health* 59, no. 3 (March 1969):485–489.

24. ———. "Sensitivity Training: An Alternative to the T-Group Method. *The Record* 71, no. 4 (May 1970):633–640. (Teachers College, Columbia University.)

25. Wiener, Norbert. *The Human Use of Human Beings.* Boston: Houghton-Mifflin Company, 1954.

26. Wolfenstein, Martha. *Children's Humor.* Glencoe, Ill.: The Free Press, 1954.

27. Wooldridge, Dean E. *The Machinery of Life.* New York: McGraw-Hill Book Company, 1966.

Chapter 6 (pages 151 to 155)

1. Eisenberg, Leon. "If Not Now, When?" *American Journal of Orthopsychiatry* 32 (1962), no. 5:781–793.

2. Glidewell, John C., and Swallow, Carolyn S. *The Prevalence of Maladjustment in Elementary Schools.* Report to the Joint Commission on Mental Health of Children. Chicago: The University of Chicago, July 1968.

3. ———. "The Professional Practitioner and His Community." Chairman's address delivered at the business meeting of the Mental Health Section, at the annual meeting of the American Public Health Association, Detroit, November 12, 1968. Reprinted in full in the APHA Mental Health Section Newsletter, January 1969.

4. Kelly, Walt. *The Pogo Papers,* Foreword. New York: Simon & Schuster, 1953.

INDEX